Overhowden and Airhouse, Scottish Borders

Characterization and interpretation of two spectacular lithic assemblages from sites near the Overhowden henge

Torben Bjarke Ballin

BAR British Series 539

2011

Published in 2016 by
BAR Publishing, Oxford

BAR British Series 539

Overhowden and Airhouse, Scottish Borders

ISBN 978 1 4073 0826 5

BAR Publishing is the trading name of British Archaeological Reports (Oxford) Ltd.
British Archaeological Reports was first incorporated in 1974 to publish the BAR
Series, International and British. In 1992 Hadrian Books Ltd became part of the BAR
group. This volume was originally published by Archaeopress in conjunction with
British Archaeological Reports (Oxford) Ltd / Hadrian Books Ltd, the Series principal
publisher, in 2011. This present volume is published by BAR Publishing, 2016.

Printed in England

BAR
PUBLISHING

BAR titles are available from:

BAR Publishing
122 Banbury Rd, Oxford, OX2 7BP, UK
EMAIL   info@barpublishing.com
PHONE   +44 (0)1865 310431
FAX   +44 (0)1865 316916
www.barpublishing.com

The present volume is dedicated to

Terry Manby

for his inspirational work on the material culture

of the British Late Neolithic period,

not least through his trail-blazing volume

Grooved Ware Sites in Yorkshire and the North of England

(BAR British Series 9, 1974)

CONTENTS

LIST OF FIGURES

LIST OF TABLES

ACKNOWLEDGEMENTS

As mentioned in the report's account of the project's history (Chapter 1), the present project was proposed to me by Dr Alison Sheridan, Head of Early Prehistory, National Museums Scotland, and I am grateful to Dr Sheridan for this opportunity to discuss a most interesting group of Late Neolithic lithic finds. I am equally grateful to National Museums Scotland, and to Keeper of Archaeology, David Clarke, for providing the necessary funding to carry out the work. Senior Curator Alan Saville, also National Museums Scotland, was the project's manager, and he was always available for discussion of lithic issues, offering much advice, as well as, towards the project's end, the necessary constructive criticism. The National Museums' photographer, Joyce Smith, photographed a selection of flints from the two sites.

In my attempt to 'get acquainted' with Yorkshire flint, I visited Terry Manby at his home in Yorkshire. He kindly offered to organize a guided tour along the Yorkshire coast, and during this field-trip we collected many samples of local flint, belonging to a number of relevant sub-types. Later, we had an improvised meeting with Peter Makey, who generously shared his knowledge on the topic, and showed me some of the region's common and less common forms of flint. When Terry had undertaken more sampling of local flint, he occasionally sent me boxes with additional specimens. It is probably an understatement to say that I would have been much less knowledgeable (in terms of Yorkshire flint, its properties and variation) without the input of Terry and Peter.

I would also like to thank Dr Randolph Donahue from Archaeological, Geographical and Environmental Sciences, University of Bradford, for examining and commenting on the use-wear of a number of interesting tool types, and Dr Benjamin Chan from Department of Archaeology, University of Sheffield, for letting me see some of his published and unpublished work on the lithics from Durrington Walls. Thanks are also owed to Mr Richard White (Hawick Museum), and Mrs Rosemary Hannay (Tweeddale Museum) for going through the museum archives in a search for 'stray' finds from Airhouse and Overhowden, and Drs Nick Card (Orkney College) and Andy Jones/Hugo Lamdin-Whymark (University of Southampton) for permission to use unpublished information on the sites of Ness of Brodgar (Orkney) and Torbhlaren (Argyll).

1. INTRODUCTION

1.1 Project background

In 2008, the author was invited by Dr Alison Sheridan, National Museums Scotland, to investigate two of the Museum's older lithic collections, the assemblages from Airhouse and Overhowden in the Scottish Borders. They were collected by James Sharp (1912) and John Fortune (Callander 1928) in the first part of the 20th Century, the Airhouse assemblage numbering 558 lithic artefacts and the Overhowden assemblage 109 lithic artefacts (Table 2.1-1). They were both collected from locations situated a few hundred metres from the Overhowden Henge (with which they may in some way be associated), and they both embrace a broad spectrum of Late Neolithic tools, with relatively sophisticated, or 'fancy', pieces being notably more prominent than in other collections from this period.

The main background to the project is the fact that, in Scotland, several interesting Late Neolithic assemblages have been recovered or written up lately (eg, Den of Boddam/Skelmuir Hill, Stoneyhill, Midmill, East Lochside, Doon Hill, and Barnhouse; Saville 2008; Suddaby & Ballin forthcoming; Ballin forthcoming h; Johnson & Ballin 2006; Middleton 2005), and south of the Anglo-Scottish border many Late Neolithic sites and landscapes have been investigated (eg, Storey's Bar Road, Tye Field, Hunstanton, Middle Harling, North Dale/South Landing, Raunds, and the Stonehenge Environs Project/ the Stonehenge Riverside project; Pryor 1978; Healy 1985; 1993; 1995; Durden 1995; Chan 2009). As a whole, this new corpus of comparative material offers a unique opportunity to gain insight into the seemingly unusual material from Airhouse/Overhowden by placing it in a wider Late Neolithic context.

1.2 Aims and objectives

The aims of the project may be subdivided into mostly descriptive objectives and mostly interpretive objectives, where the former provide the foundation for the latter. The first and most basic objective is to characterize the Airhouse and Overhowden assemblages in terms of typology, technology and raw material use to allow the definition and understanding of 1) distinctive Late Neolithic types; 2) typical Late Neolithic technological approaches; and 3) Late Neolithic raw material preferences.

The typological characterization of the finds (Chapter 2.3) includes discussions of the most important lithic tool types from the Late Neolithic period, such as the chisel-shaped and oblique arrowheads, the knife forms, the scrapers, the

polished-edge implements, the piercers, the strike-a-lights (or 'fabricators'), the serrated pieces, and the combined tools. A more precise Late Neolithic typology may provide greater understanding of the function of the period's tool types as well as allow more reliable comparison of the period's assemblages and sites.

The technological section (Chapter 2.4) primarily focuses on the Levallois-like technology, which (apart from related approaches dating to the British and European Middle Palaeolithic) is unique to this period, and which is still relatively poorly understood, or even misunderstood (basically, perceived as simple, where it is in fact quite sophisticated). The understanding of the raw material preferences at Airhouse/Overhowden – in essence, the dominance of exotic flint, probably from the greater Yorkshire area – may prove essential to the understanding of those sites' position in Late Neolithic society via their links with more remote parts of the British Isles (Chapter 3).

Following the characterization of the Airhouse/ Overhowden material, the combined assemblage is compared with other Late Neolithic assemblages from the British Isles, first and foremost to allow those two sites to be defined in relation to the Overhowden Henge, as well as in relation to other Late Neolithic sites. Are the sites of Airhouse and Overhowden 'special' in any sense, or do they simply represent extremes of a 'normal' continuum? Elements essential to the comparative analysis are:

1. Numerical assemblage size (how numerically large are the two assemblages compared to other Late Neolithic assemblages?);
2. Raw material composition (what is the proportion of exotic lithic material compared to locally procured material?);
3. General artefact composition (what are the relative proportions of the main artefact categories, debitage, cores and tools?);
4. The composition of the tools (what are the relative ratios of the individual tool categories and which proportion of the tools appear to be 'fancy'); and
5. Macroscopic use-wear (do the recovered implements appear to have been used and if so, how much?).

By comparing the Airhouse and Overhowden assemblages with other British assemblages from the period, it will be attempted to characterize the two parent sites in terms of site function. The available archaeological literature suggests that British Late Neolithic society may have included the following general site types (although hybrid forms are likely to exist), which may be characterized by different forms of lithic assemblages:

1. Extraction sites, where raw material was either mined or collected, and where core and tool rough-outs may have been prepared;
2. Domestic settlements;
3. Settlements functionally linked to ritual sites (eg, builders of henges, 'care-taker sites', locations of some rituals of relevance to the general activities at the ritual sites);
4. Ritual sites (henges, stone circles and rock art sites); and
5. Burials

In Chapter 3.4, the lithic finds from Airhouse and Overhowden are compared with selected assemblages from sites of the categories listed above.

1.3 Airhouse and Overhowden

The two assemblages were recovered from two areas near the Overhowden Henge, namely Airhouse Farm and Overhowden Farm. The Airhouse assemblage was collected mainly by John Robert Fortune, the then owner of Airhouse Farm, who presented the finds to National Museums Scotland (Callander 1928). The flints were collected in the immediate surroundings of the farm, which lies on the western slopes of Lauderdale, near the head of the valley, at an elevation of approximately 330 m. To the north, the ground falls quickly towards the Mountmill Burn, whereas to the east and south the descent is more gradual. To the west, the land rolls up to a height of 4-500 m before it suddenly descends into Gala Water about six km distant. The distance to the Overhowden Henge towards the south-south-east just exceeds one km.

Most of the Overhowden assemblage was collected by James Sharp (1912) from a location 2-300 m north of the henge, although some were gathered less than 100 m from the monument, and individual artefacts were found inside the henge and south of it. The area with the henge and the find-spot is at an elevation of approximately 300 m, on fairly level ground. Towards the west, the ground gently rolls up to a height of 350 m (a northern extension of Collie Law), whereas towards the east it descends into Leader Water, about two km away. A few hundred metres north and south of the site, the ground falls towards two small east-west orientated burns. According to Atkinson (1950, 62), most of the finds were made on a small eminence facing the henge entrance (see below). Trial excavations were undertaken in this area in the autumn of 1950 but revealed nothing, and Atkinson suggests that '... *it is probable that the process of cultivation which exposed the numerous flints has also destroyed any structures with which they may have been associated*'.

As indicated in connection with the characterization and discussion of the finds, the assemblages are clearly the products of selection, either in the field or after collection or, more likely, both. Although the collection of artefacts in the field is likely to have disregarded smaller and less impressive finds, more debitage and cores must have been recovered. The question is whether those have been lost, or whether they still exist as parts of local farm or museum collections. In connection with the present project, Hawick Museum and Tweeddale Museum, both in the Scottish Borders, were contacted, and enquiries were made as to whether finds from the general Overhowden area might have been offered to their collections in the past. Apparently, no finds in Tweeddale Museum derive from the Airhouse and Overhowden sites, and in Hawick Museum only one chisel-shaped arrowhead from Overhowden was found (ETLMS 2941).

The two Late Neolithic sites are likely to be at least partly contemporary with the Overhowden Henge, and it is quite likely that their high yield of above-average quality (and thereby probably higher prestige) lithic objects is due to special functions relating to this monument. Although some of the English giant henges have produced notable quantities of usually well-executed flint artefacts (eg, Durrington Walls; Wainwright & Longworth 1971; Chan forthcoming), henges are generally known for their low yield of finds (Chapter 3.2.4), whereas sites in the immediate vicinity of these monuments may produce more – and more impressive – flints than average Late Neolithic settlements (Chapter 3.2.3).

The Overhowden Henge, approximately 150 m west of Overhowden Farm, was briefly described by Atkinson (1950, 59) in a paper on recently discovered henge monuments from Scotland and Northumberland. He classified the new henges according to whether they have a single entrance (Class I) or two entrances (Class II). The Overhowden Henge has one entrance. Prior to excavations in 1949 by Stuart Piggott, and in 1950 by Atkinson himself, the monument had been registered and mapped as a fort, but the investigations clearly showed that it had the same attributes as Britain's well-known henges. It has an external bank and two concentric ditches, a broad outer ditch and a narrow inner ditch. It measures approximately 110 m from bank to bank, and at the time of the excavations, the height of the bank was *c.* 30 cm. Since then, the height of the monument has been lowered further by continued ploughing.

1.4 Definition of the Late Neolithic period

In British archaeological literature, the Late Neolithic period is usually defined in two different ways, depending on the perspective of the individual analyst: pottery specialists tend to define the period in one way, and lithics specialists in another. In an attempt to clarify matters, both definitions are presented and discussed below.

The ceramic perspective ('the Late Neolithic sensu stricto'): This perspective is shared by most pottery specialists (eg, Gibson 2002, 78, 83) who tend to define the Late Neolithic as the period during which Grooved Ware pottery was in use (mostly 3100–26/2500 cal BC, but with some possible later survivals), whereas the related Impressed Ware material (3500–2900, but mainly 3300–3000 cal BC) is perceived as representing the later part of the Early Neolithic period (dates courtesy of Dr Alison Sheridan, National Museums Scotland). Megaw & Simpson (1979) appear to have positioned themselves between two stools, as they incorporate Grooved Ware and Impressed Ware groups within their later Neolithic period, but they also write that the '... *Peterborough styles [ie, Impressed Ware] [...] appear to be simply a pottery tradition rather than one aspect of a distinctive Late Neolithic culture, whereas the further associations of stone and bone equipment and monuments with Rinyo-Claction Grooved Ware do suggest the ceramic element in a recognizable archaeological culture*' (ibid., 166).

The lithic perspective ('the Late Neolithic sensu largo): The presently available lithic evidence clearly supports a broader definition of the Late Neolithic as a period when Impressed Ware as well as Grooved Ware were in use. In lithic terms, this extended Late Neolithic period represents a break with traditional Early Neolithic flint work, including artefact morphology, lithic technology, raw material preferences, exchange patterns, and practices of deposition (contra Megaw & Simpson 1979; above). These topics are all discussed in greater detail below (Chapter 1.5), and the following should only be perceived as a brief summary of British Late Neolithic lithic traditions.

In terms of artefact morphology, the most emblematic Late Neolithic tool form is the *petit tranchet* derivative arrowhead (from this point onwards abbreviated to PTD; Clark 1934b). The shift from leaf-shaped arrowheads to chisel-shaped arrowheads probably takes place in the early stages of the Impressed Ware period, with some kite-shaped (ie, late leaf-shaped) arrowheads also dating to this time (Green 1980, 85; Clarke *et al.* 1985, 63-67). Oblique arrowheads are introduced later, and PTDs are generally phased out before the beginning of the Early Bronze Age. In his report on the lithic finds from Raunds in Northamptonshire, the author wrote (Ballin forthcoming d):

'*At Hunstanton a number of chisel-shaped arrowheads were associated with Grooved Ware (Healy et al. 1993, 34), suggesting that the general perception of chisel-shaped arrowheads being associated with Peterborough Ware and oblique arrowheads with Grooved Ware may be an over-simplification (cf. discussion in Saville 1981, 49-50). This notion is further supported by the material from pits at Fengate, where chisel-shaped and oblique arrowheads were found together (eg. Pit W17; Pryor 1978, 104-5), and Green (1980, 235-6) has documented the association of chisel-shaped arrowheads with the Clacton*

and Woodlands sub-styles. Probably, oblique arrowheads [date] exclusively [to Grooved Ware contexts], whereas the simpler forms of the transverse arrowhead may appear in Peterborough Ware (later fourth millennium) as well as Grooved Ware [...] contexts'.

The Late Neolithic 'typological package', which was introduced during the first stages of the Impressed Ware period, also included technological innovation, and most of this period, as well as, apparently, the entire Grooved Ware period, is characterized by the use of the highly specialized Levallois-like technique (Ballin forthcoming a; discussed in greater detail in Chapter 2.4.1-2). In a number of papers (eg, Ballin forthcoming d), the author characterized Late Neolithic flint work as representing a flake industry, but subsequent investigation of this technological approach (eg, Suddaby & Ballin forthcoming; Ballin forthcoming a; the present report) clearly shows that it is a blade-and-flake technique, and that blades are only phased out in the later stages of the Late Neolithic.

Scottish Impressed Ware sites, as well as Grooved Ware sites, are characterized not only by the use of the Levallois-like approach, but also by the heavy reliance on exotic, so-called Yorkshire flint (Chapters 2.2; 2.5.1). This flint tends to be in either marbled grey or homogenous dark-brown colours, and it seems to dominate areas like the Scottish Borders, the Lothian counties, and South Lanarkshire entirely (eg, Stevenson 1948), whereas Early Neolithic assemblages from south-east Scotland tend to be dominated by local flint and/or chert. Further afield, the frequency of Yorkshire flint drops somewhat, but even on Orkney the period's best pieces (arrowheads, 'fancy' knives, etc.) are in this material (eg, the Barnhouse assemblage; examined by the author at Orkney Museum). Most likely, as suggested below, Yorkshire flint is introduced gradually during the later stages of the Early Neolithic, and it is still in use during the first stages of the Early Bronze Age.

The introduction of exotic flint from north-east England signals changing exchange relations and exchange forms. As explained in Ballin (2009), the first half of the Early Neolithic period was characterized by a west-east going exchange of Arran pitchstone, which dropped to a trickle in the second half of the period. In the second half of the Early Neolithic period, probably towards the period's end, the exchange in lithic raw materials changed direction from west-east to east-west. By the beginning of the Impressed Ware period, pitchstone was no longer exchanged outside the Arran/Argyll & Bute region (and Orkney), and the exchange in lithic raw materials now focused entirely on Yorkshire flint (through the Neolithic period some flint was imported from Antrim, but apparently never in the volumes observed in connection with the importation of Yorkshire flint; this, however, ought to be the focus of a separate investigation). These social changes also embraced practices of deposition, as for example experienced in connection with changes from communal burials to individual burials.

Most likely, the ceramic-based definition of the Late Neolithic period was founded on the scarcity (until recently) of well-dated, representative later Neolithic lithic assemblages and, after the addition of much new evidence, it should be abandoned. The two ceramic (Impressed Ware and Grooved Ware) periods are both characterized by a common – and distinctive – lithic tradition (associated with distinctive social forms), which sets them apart from the preceding Early Neolithic period.

As mentioned in Saville (2006, 1), attempts are periodically made to introduce a British Middle Neolithic period, but '... *these subdivisions are only possible to apply with any success to certain regions of Britain, where there is more abundant and specific better-quality relevant evidence to substantiate them. [...] Even in [these] cases, however, it is difficult to identify specifically Middle Neolithic lithic types [...]*' (ibid., 2).

1.5   British Late Neolithic lithics

The purpose of this chapter is not to list all Late Neolithic sites from Britain or all British papers in which Late Neolithic lithics have been discussed, but to highlight key achievements on the way towards expanding our understanding of Late Neolithic lithics. This work has mainly focused on three areas, namely 1) typology; 2) technology; and 3) raw material procurement (eg, flint mining and exchange).

1.5.1 Late Neolithic lithic typology

The typological work was spearheaded by J.G.D. Clark, who in the first half of the 20th Century produced a series of papers which attempted to define some of the period's iconic tool types (Clark 1932a-b; 1934b). Although some of these tool types have been touched upon in later papers (below), Clark's papers are still the main points of reference relating to Late Neolithic lithics. The most significant of Clark's papers on Late Neolithic implements is, beyond doubt, his discussion of the British *Petit Tranchet* derivative arrowheads, or PTDs, which include the so-called chisel-shaped and oblique arrowheads. As mentioned in Chapter 2.3.1, this work was to a large extent based on formal intuition, rather than context and association, but Clark's typology remains a useful one.

The British PTDs were discussed by Green (1980, 30, 100; 1984; 25) in his work on British Neolithic and Bronze Age lithic arrowheads but, as mentioned below (Chapter 2.3.1), it is this author's view that Green may have over-simplified matters somewhat and possibly 'thrown the baby out with the bath-water'. He carried out metric analyses of the PTDs, and reached the conclusion that two basic forms exist, the chisel-shaped and oblique arrowheads, where the former were used as transverse arrowheads and the latter as pointed arrowheads. But as shown in Chapter 2.3.1, the situation may be slightly more complex. Basically, Green's simplified classification makes it very difficult to

discuss the morphological development of the sub-types and therefore also their possible levels of diagnosticity and function (not only how these arrowheads were hafted but also whether simple and well-executed specimens were deposited in different contexts). However, one of the biggest problems in terms of working with Clark's types is probably their relatively loose definitions, and future work – for example following the publication of recent finds from Durrington Wall – ought to aim at tightening the PTD classification system.

Apart from Green's discussion of the PTDs, no archaeologists have attempted to discuss, constructively critizice, adjust or add to Clark's various classification systems. In general, excavators and analysts have simply followed Clark's original (to a degree, subjective) typologies when they presented new assemblages. This has produced a string of useful publications in which it has, on occasion, been possible to discuss the find circumstances and contexts of the Late Neolithic types.

These publications include, *inter alia*, Smith's (1965) presentation of the finds from the Late Neolithic contexts at Windmill Hill in Wiltshire (Keiller's excavations 1925-39), as well as those from West Kennet Avenue, Wiltshire; Wainwright & Longworth's (1971) presentation of the finds from the Durrington Walls Henge in Wiltshire (excavations 1966-68), with the publication including an overview of Late Neolithic artefacts and PTDs from other Late Neolithic sites in England; Healy's (1985) presentation of the finds from the ring-ditch at Tye Field in Essex, which provides an overview of a typical later Late Neolithic assemblage and compares it with British Early Neolithic, Late Neolithic and Early Bronze Age assemblages; and Pryor's (1978) presentation of the finds from the Grooved Ware settlement of Storey's Bar Road at Fengate in Norfolk provides excellent documentation of contexts (such as pits) where chisel-shaped and oblique arrowheads occur together. Other useful reports are Healy's discussion of the finds from Hunstanton (1993), Middle Harling (1995) and the Wissey Embayment (1996), all Norfolk, which offer further comparative material.

Apart from Clark's and Green's productions, only Manby's (1974) volume on the Grooved Ware sites of Yorkshire can be characterized as providing frontline typological information on Late Neolithic lithics. In addition to presenting a catalogue of Grooved Ware assemblages from north-east England, Manby also lists typical Late Neolithic tool forms, and although it is not possible to characterize his typological work as an actual classification system, his illustrations of discoidal knives, polished-edge knives and polished-edge implements from Yorkshire provide an excellent overview of these categories.

Saville (1981) presents a discussion of 'rods' from Grimes Graves in Norfolk (1971/72 excavations). Healy's (1996, 76) inclusion of some of those in her definition of Late Neolithic strike-a-lights/fabricators is slightly misleading, as the excavator (Saville pers. comm.) is adamant that – due to the general absence of terminal abrasion – they do not form part of this category. The Grimes Graves pieces are probably mainly associated with the Middle Bronze Age activities at this location, and their likely Bronze Age date may explain why the Grimes Graves 'rods' differ somewhat from the typical Late Neolithic strike-a-lights from, for example, Airhouse/Overhowden: the former are mainly based on transverse sections of thick flakes, whereas the latter are generally based on elongated flakes and stout blades. Pierpoint's (1980, 124) discussion of British plano-convex knives does not add anything to the understanding of this type in typological and technological terms, but the many illustrated specimens are helpful to analysts dealing with Late Neolithic flint knives.

1.5.2 Late Neolithic lithic technology

Apparently, Late Neolithic flint-working took several forms, with some assemblages being based predominantly on traditional techniques (hard percussion and bipolar approaches), whereas others are based almost exclusively on the Levallois-like technique (Chapter 2.4.1-2). Traditional reduction techniques have been discussed at length elsewhere (eg, Inizan *et al.* 1992, 58), and the present chapter therefore only deals with the identification and explanation of the British Levallois-like approach.

Due to similarities between the Middle Palaeolithic Levalloisian technique and the Late Neolithic Levallois-like technique, discussions of the former were helpful in gaining an understanding of the latter. Particularly Roe's (1981, 79) discussion of the Levalloisian, which he emphasizes is a *technique* and not a *period*, was useful. In this paper, he gives a step-by-step overview of the Levalloisian reduction process, the main steps of which correspond to those of the Levallois-like approach (Chapters 2.4.1-2). This approach is also discussed at length in Inizan *et al.* (1992, 48) and Kuhn (1995, 83).

The post-Palaeolithic date of typical Levallois-like waste products, such as the tortoise core rough-outs and the Levallois-like cores, was not realized until typical Late Neolithic assemblages were published, combining these waste products with diagnostic Late Neolithic tool forms. Moore's (1963) paper on the finds from Beacon Hill in East Yorkshire was the first step in this direction. Despite obvious dating problems (the assemblage is subdivided into a small Neolithic sub-assemblage and a much larger Early Bronze Age assemblage, where it is now clear that probably most of the flints date to the Late Neolithic), this collection combines 'tortoise cores' and PTDs, thus suggesting a date after the Palaeolithic era. Other typical Late Neolithic flint artefacts at Beacon Hill are axehead rough-outs, unpolished axeheads, blade-scrapers, horseshoe-scrapers, one plano-convex knife, fragments of discoidal knives, and finely serrated blades and flakes. The site's pottery included Early Neolithic forms, Peterborough Ware, Grooved Ware and Beaker sherds.

An important step towards a fuller understanding of this technique, its associated attributes, and its date, was taken by Manby (1974, 83) in his synthetic work on the Grooved Ware settlements of Yorkshire. He noticed that many Late Neolithic flakes and blades have finely faceted platform remnants and suggested that this was due to the application of a technique similar to the Middle Palaeolithic Levalloisian.

Since the publication of Manby's work, these cores and their products have been reported from Late Neolithic sites throughout Britain, and they were discussed by Saville (1981, 44-48) in connection with his examination of the Late Neolithic and later Bronze Age assemblages from the flint mines at Grimes Graves in Norfolk. Over the last few decades, Levallois-like cores have been recovered from Late Neolithic settlement sites in East Anglia (eg, Healy 1993; 1996), with further supplements from Yorkshire (eg, Durden 1995). They have also been encountered on Late Neolithic sites throughout Scotland, where they were retrieved from procurement sites, settlement sites, and ritual sites (Chapters 2.4 and 3.2).

1.5.3 Raw material procurement

Throughout the British Neolithic, the procurement of flint took two main forms, namely surface collection and mining. The collection of flint was carried out from whatever sources were available at the surface (which could be beach flint, flint from watercourses, as well as flint eroding out of fields), whereas flint mining followed primary seams (as in southern and eastern England) or derived sources (as in north-east Scotland) underground. In the archaeological literature, Neolithic flint mining in general has been dealt with on numerous occasions (eg, Barber *et al.* 1999; Russell 2000).

Many of the English mines were exploited in the Early Neolithic period and most were abandoned by the onset of the Grooved Ware period, or shortly thereafter (eg, Harrow Hill, Church Hill, Blackpatch and Cissbury; Barber *et al.* 1999, Fig. 1.2). However, exploitation of the flint at Grimes Graves in Norfolk was initiated around the beginning of the Grooved Ware period (ibid.), and the most extensive quarrying at this location took place during this period, with some mining continuing into the Early Bronze Age. Flint was still being procured from the mines at Grimes Graves by the Middle Bronze Age but, by then, primarily in the form of scavenging of the Late Neolithic spoil heaps. For discussion of the individual early mines, see Russell 2000 (with extensive bibliography).

The largest of all Neolithic flint mining areas in Britain, and the one mostly associated with Late Neolithic operations, is Grimes Graves. This is also the most extensively excavated Neolithic mining area. The most significant early campaigns are those of Peake (eg, 1917) and Armstrong (eg, 1926; 1934). An important topic of the early work was the date of the mining at Grimes

Graves, with for example Armstrong strongly advocating a Palaeolithic date. This was argued against by, among others, Clark & Piggott (1933), who suggested a Neolithic date.

In the early 1970s, the Department of Environment, under the leadership of Roger Mercer, undertook renewed excavations in the area, with several shafts being excavated and their structural elements and finds analysed in great detail. The finds from the 1971-72 shafts were examined and discussed by Saville (1981), whereas those from Shaft X were dealt with by Herne (1991). Unfortunately, these reports focused largely on the sites' Bronze Age element, although Saville's contribution includes valuable discussions of the Levallois-like approach and its associated finely faceted butts, as well as differences in composition between assemblages deposited by people in the Late Neolithic and Middle Bronze Age periods (Saville 1981, 6).

No flint mining appears to have taken place in Yorkshire, probably due to the hardness of the local chalk, but the Yorkshire outcrops and the Late Neolithic collection of flint in this area are discussed in Durden (1995, 410). Her analysis of two Late Neolithic sites, and their different compositions and approaches to lithic reduction, led her to suggest that some degree of specialization had taken place: most probably, South Landing was one of several extraction sites which supplied raw material and tool rough-outs to specialist flint-knappers at North Dale (ibid., 431). Gardiner's (2008, 242) research into Late Neolithic discoidal knives implies a similar scenario for East Sussex. A project looking into the Yorkshire flint sources (for example characterizing and discussing the area's individual flint types and their likely occurrences) would be highly useful.

In 1994-95, Alan Saville, National Museums Scotland, carried out excavations at two prehistoric mining sites near Peterhead in Aberdeenshire: Den of Boddam and Skelmuir Hill (Bridgland *et al.* 1995; Saville 1995; 2005; 2006). The quarrying operations in this area were associated with an extensive deposit of derived inland flint, the Buchan Ridge Gravels, and they are probably largely of a Late Neolithic date. Ongoing examination and analysis of the approximately one million recovered artefacts suggest that, at these sites, blanks were produced mainly by Levallois-like approaches, with bipolar technique having been applied mainly in the initial stages ('quartering'), or to reduce disintegrated nodules and cores (Saville forthcoming).

The procurement of flint in the Late Neolithic period was more than simply a practical undertaking, where knappable flint was obtained in sufficient quantities. As demonstrated in connection with ethno-archaeological work (eg, Scott & Thiessen 2005), it usually had a religious or spiritual side, where the lithic raw material was associated with, for example, totemic entities and, as a consequence, the quarrying operations formed part of a chain of events, which involved prescribed rituals. Topping (2005) has produced a model for the possible social context of flint mining at Grimes Graves, based on evidence from Shaft 27.

Another equally important aspect of the procurement process was the exchange in mined or collected lithic material, where for example flint was transported from the sources to, frequently, distant 'end-users'. The Late Neolithic exchange network responsible for the dissemination of Yorkshire flint has never been the topic of detailed discussion, but a similar, slightly earlier network was considered in the author's (2009) volume on the Early Neolithic 'Arran Pitchstone Interaction Sphere'. In this monograph, the exchange of Scottish pitchstone ($\approx$ obsidian) was discussed with reference to, among other things, the extensive American Hopewell Interaction Sphere (eg, Caldwell 1964; Struever & Houart 1972; Yerkes 2002). The author's examination of Late Neolithic assemblages from Scotland indicates that the Scottish Late Neolithic exchange in flint may have differed from the Early Neolithic pitchstone exchange in many respects (direction, volume, socio-economical mechanisms, etc.). However, there are still too few representative Late Neolithic assemblages available to allow the sort of analysis carried out on the Scottish pitchstone exchange, and investigation of the Late Neolithic exchange of Yorkshire flint into Scotland is therefore a task for the future.

2. THE OVERHOWDEN AND AIRHOUSE ASSEMBLAGES

2.1   Overview of the finds

The two assemblages from Airhouse and Overhowden include a total of 667 lithic artefacts, with the Airhouse collection numbering 558 pieces and the Overhowden collection 109 pieces. Table 1 offers a complete typological overview of the finds, whereas Table 2 represents a summary list of the main finds categories.

The general composition of the assemblages clearly shows that they represent a selection, with tools amounting to 96%. In contrast to the recovery of 643 tools, only 21 unmodified blanks seem to have been found, supplemented by three Levallois-like cores (Figs 1a-b). It would be almost impossible to produce assemblages with such a skewed composition in the field, suggesting that some selection took place after recovery. The finder may have offered or sold these artefacts to a local museum (although contacts to local museums have shown that the most obvious local museums, in Hawick and Peebles, have only received one chisel-shaped arrowhead from the Overhowden area between them; Chapter 1.3) or local collectors, and an attempt should be made to locate them. The absence of these less visually pleasing objects makes it difficult to establish how large a proportion of the combined Airhouse/ Overhowden assemblage was produced on-site, and how many pieces may have been brought to the sites from other locations. If this is not possible, it is suggested to undertake future sampling at Airhouse and Overhowden, for example in the form of limited test-pitting, simply to gauge whether substantial amounts of debitage may still be present (Chapter 4).

Table 2 presents a clearer picture of the typological differences between the two assemblages than the more detailed Table 1. In relative terms, the Overhowden collection has almost twice as many Late Neolithic arrowheads as that of Airhouse (55% vs 34%), whereas the Airhouse collection has almost twice as many scrapers as that of Overhowden (30% vs 16%). At present, it is not possible to say whether the absence of combined or serrated tools in the Overhowden assemblage is a reality, or whether it reflects a recovery or post-recovery bias. The most obvious difference between these assemblages and other Late Neolithic assemblages from Scotland is the impressive numbers of arrowheads, but some individual tool types, like invasively retouched knives, polished-edge implements, and strike-a-lights are usually also less common than at Airhouse and Overhowden (see Chapter 3.2).

In the following chapters, the two assemblages are mostly dealt with *en bloc* and referred to as the Airhouse/

Overhowden assemblage (compositional differences are shown in Tables 1 and 2) – they are only treated separately when obvious differences need to be discussed. The typological section only deals with the two sites' implements, whereas debitage and cores are discussed in the technological section on the basis of the two sites' tool blanks.

2.2   Raw material preferences

The lithic finds from Airhouse and Overhowden are mainly in flint (95% and 98%, respectively), supplemented by chert (5% and 2%, respectively) and minuscule amounts of chalcedony (one leaf-shaped arrowhead from Airhouse) and pitchstone (three pieces from Airhouse) (Table 1). The distribution of the chert across artefact categories suggests that this raw material may mainly be associated with Early Neolithic activities at the two sites and, to a smaller degree, Early Bronze Age activities. Only one PTD is in chert (*c.* 0.5%), whereas one-third (34%) of the leaf-shaped arrowheads are in this material, and one-tenth (11%) of the barbed-and-tanged arrowheads. Apart from two arrowheads in chert (one leaf-shaped and one barbed-and-tanged point), the Overhowden material includes no tools in this material, whereas the assemblage from Airhouse includes substantially higher numbers of chert tools: 13 arrowheads (11 leaf-shaped and two barbed-and-tanged points), one scale-flaked knife, seven scrapers, and three pieces with invasive retouch or edge-retouch.

Mesolithic assemblages from south-east Scotland were examined in the stores of National Museums Scotland (also see Corrie 1916; Callander 1927; Mason 1931; Mulholland 1970), and they generally include considerable amounts of red, yellow, orange and honey-brown flints, which are thought to represent local pebble flint collected along the North Sea shores of the Scottish Borders. In contrast, the flint artefacts from Airhouse and Overhowden are predominantly in grey and dark-brown colours, which Mulholland (1970; 85) suggested may have been imported from north-east England. Only 36 of 629 pieces (6%) in flint are not grey or dark-brown, but cream (18 pieces), yellow/orange (seven pieces), pink (six pieces, possibly burnt), red (three pieces) or 'other' (two pieces). Six clearly fire-crazed pieces are white.

The assemblages from Airhouse and Overhowden differ considerably in terms of their relative numbers of grey and dark-brown artefacts (Table 3). The finds from Airhouse are heavily dominated by greys (80%), with dark-brown pieces being relatively uncommon (14%), whereas the finds from Overhowden are also dominated by greys (57%) but include substantially higher proportions of

	Airhouse			Overhowden		
	Flint	Chert	Other raw materials	Flint	Chert	Total
Debitage						
Flakes	7	2				9
Blades	5	2	1	1		9
Microblades					2	2
Indeterminate pieces					1	1
Total debitage	12	4	1	1	3	21
Cores						
Levallois-like cores	3					3
Total cores	3					3
Tools						
Leaf-shaped arrowheads	19	11	1	3	1	35
Petit tranchet derivative arrowheads	183	1		58		242
Barbed-and-tanged arrowheads	18	2		5	1	26
Edge-polished adzeheads	1					1
Backed knives	1					1
Scale-flaked knives	30	1		4		35
Plano-convex knives	3			1		4
Discoidal knives	1					1
Polished-edge knives				1		1
Discoidal scrapers	6	1		1		8
Short end-scrapers	98	5		10		113
Blade-scrapers	4			3		7
Double-scrapers	6					6
Double-scrapers/side-scrapers	2					2
Side-scrapers	17	1		2		20
Side-/end-scrapers	18			1		19
Concave scrapers	1					1
Scraper-edge fragments	3					3
Polished-edge end-scrapers	13			4		17
Polished-edge side-scrapers	2					2
Polished-edge retouched pieces	2					2
Strike-a-lights	6			2		8
Piercers	9			2		11
Serrated pieces	2					2
Saws	3					3
Combined tools (knives/scrapers)	7					7
Combined tools (knives/piercers)	6					6
Combined tools (knives/strike-a-lights)	1					1
Combined tools (knives/polished-edges)	3					3
Pieces w curved truncations				1		1
Pieces w oblique truncations	1					1
Pieces w retouched notches	1			1		2
Burins	1					1
Indeterminate bifacial implements				2		2
Indeterminate implements	1					1
Fragments w invasive retouch	4	2				6
Pieces w edge-retouch, flint	36	1	2	2		41
Gunflints	1					1
Total tools	510	25	3	103	2	643
GRAND TOTAL	525	29	4	104	5	667

Table 1. General artefact list.

Figs 1a-b. The worked upper face (the flaking-front) and the unworked lower face of a Levallois-like core from Airhouse (BMA 643).

	Quantity			Per cent		
	Airhouse	*Overhowden*	*Total*	*Airhouse*	*Overhowden*	*Total*
LN Arrowheads	184	58	242	34	55	38
Other arrowheads	51	10	61	10	9	9
Adzeheads	1		1	-		-
Knives	36	6	42	7	6	7
Scrapers	162	17	179	30	16	28
Polished-edge implements	17	4	21	3	4	3
Piercers	9	2	11	2	2	2
Strike-a-lights	6	2	8	1	2	1
Serrated pieces/saws	5		5	1		1
Combined tools	17		17	3		3
Other tool forms	49	6	55	9	6	8
TOTAL	**537**	**105**	**642**	**100**	**100**	**100**

Table 2. Summary artefact list – prehistoric tools (total less one gunflint).

	Quantity					Per cent				
	Greys	*Dark-browns*	*Others*	*Burnt*	*Total*	*Greys*	*Dark-browns*	*Others*	*Burnt*	*Total*
Airhouse	420	72	27	6	*525*	80	14	5	1	*100*
Overhowden	59	36	9	0	*104*	57	35	8		*100*
TOTAL	**479**	**108**	**36**	**6**	*629*	**76**	**17**	**6**	**1**	*100*

Table 3. The flint forms recovered at Airhouse and Overhowden.

	Quantity				Per cent			
	Marbled	*Small-dotted*	*Homogeneous*	*Total*	*Marbled*	*Small-dotted*	*Homogeneous*	*Total*
Greys	360	103	16	479	75	21	4	100
Dark-browns	22	5	81	108	20	5	75	100
TOTAL	**382**	**108**	**97**	**587**	**65**	**18**	**17**	**100**

Table 4. The colours and patterning of the recovered grey and dark-brown flints.

PANEL 1: Clark's (1934b) PTD sub-forms – definitions and suggestions

Class A

Blank: Medial segment of parallel-sided flake or blade with roughly parallel dorsal arrises.

Shape: Rectangular to trapezoidal.

Retouch: Steep ('almost vertical') edge-retouch of the two snapped edges; occasionally, a third edge is worked; at least one edge (the cutting-edge) is an original lateral flake-edge; no secondary (invasive) flaking of the two faces.

Class B

Blank: Medial segment of parallel-sided flake or blade with roughly parallel dorsal arrises; occasionally, slightly less parallel flake laterals and dorsal arrises.

Shape: Clearly trapezoidal.

Retouch: Slightly flatter edge-retouch, on occasion approaching semi-invasive retouch; frequently, one or more edges are retouched from both faces.

Class C

Blank: Simple flake. Clark writes: 'We find that the sharp edge is now frequently formed by the intersection on one face of several flake scars, all the flakes having, however, been removed previous to the striking of the primary flakes from which the implement as a whole has been made'. In modern lithic terminology, this means that the dorsal faces of Class C arrowheads are characterized mainly by the intersecting, multi-directional negative flake scars from prior detachments, and where only a limited number of flake scars represent secondary invasive retouch.

Shape: Sub-triangular. <u>Class C1</u>: The cutting-edge is shorter than the modified edges. <u>Class C2</u>: The cutting-edge is longer than the modified edges.

Retouch: With Class C, the encroachment of the secondary modification of the arrowheads onto the dorsal, and to a degree ventral, faces become more marked.

Class D

Blank: Simple flake.

Shape: The first class with a marked concavity in one retouched side, having the effect of making the form asymmetrical.

Retouch: Like C.

Class E-F

Blank: Simple flake.

Shape and retouch: Clark: '[The features of Class D are ...] progressively accentuated in the Classes E and F'. The examination of the pieces from Airhouse/Overhowden showed that pieces with totally covering invasive retouch (bifacial pieces, some with sharp cutting-edges, some with secondary retouch even of that part) may be found in all the Classes E-I (oblique arrowheads).

Class G

Blank: Simple flake.

Shape: According to Clark, : 'In each of [Classes G-I], the sharp primary edge survives' (this is only partly true – some cutting-edges were sharpened or straightened by partial retouch). In Class G, the cutting-edge is roughly equal in length with the longer of the two modified edges.

Retouch: According to Clark, this Class includes most of the ripple-flaked specimens. However, at Airhouse/Overhowden, all ripple-flaked specimens (four) belong to Class H.

Class H-I

Blank: Simple flake.

Shape: Marked asymmetry (ie, with one accentuated lateral barb), for which reason these points have been referred to as 'lop-sided'. Where the cutting-edge of Class G is roughly as long as the longest modified edge, that of Class H is longer than this modified edge, and that of Class I is shorter.

Comments and suggestions

In most respects, Clarks definitions of the various classes (Panel 1, Fig. 1) are fairly general, and as he puts it himself, '... there is no more difference between Classes G and F than between Classes D-F'. Basically, the entire sequence from Class A to Class I represents a continuum, which frequently makes it necessary for the lithics analyst to operate with a number of hybrid forms.

Clark's very basic definitions, in conjunction with his illustrations, have introduced several misunderstandings. It is for example the author's impression, based on his consultation of the archaeological literature, that most specialists perceive Class C2 as a generally symmetrical (isosceles) form, and Class G as a type characterized by a slightly concave base (primarily based on Clark's illustrations of the two forms). However, this is not supported by the text of Clark's paper. In his paper, Class C2 is mainly defined by the cutting-edge being longer than the two modified edges, and Class G as having a cutting-edge as long as the longest modified edge.

As Panel 1, Fig. 2 shows, these definitions allow considerable formal variation, and some C2 forms may be slightly scalene whereas others are exceedingly scalene (however, this asymmetry is not caused by a lateral concavity, as in the case of Class D). As also shown in Panel 1, Fig. 2, some G forms may have straight bases, whereas others may have slightly convex bases.

This level of variation is supported by the examination of the finds from Airhouse/Overhowden, as well as by the investigation of other Late Neolithic assemblages from Scotland. Most Late Neolithic pitchstone arrowheads in Arran Museum, for example, are Class G points with slightly convex bases.

This increased variation makes it much more difficult to classify, characterize and date these arrowheads precisely:

There is certainly a formal overlap between the most scalene C2 points and some G forms (eg, Panel 1, Fig. 2.5 and Panel 1, Fig. 2.II);

Use-wear indicates that the approximately isosceles C2s may be chisel-shaped arrowheads, whereas the more scalene forms may have been hafted as tipped arrowheads; and

Some G forms with convex bases may be confused with leaf-shaped pieces, whereas some G forms with concave bases may, erroneously, be identified as Early Bronze Age hollow-based points.

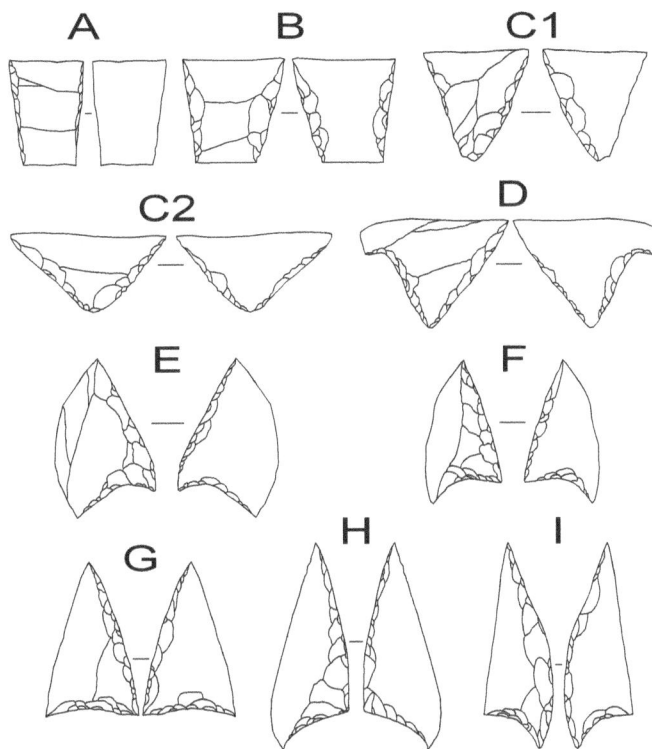

Panel 1, Fig. 1. Clark's 10 main PTD forms. Types E and F have been rotated to bring their orientation into line with present consensus on their likely hafting form. Re-drawn from Clark (1934b, Figs 1-2).

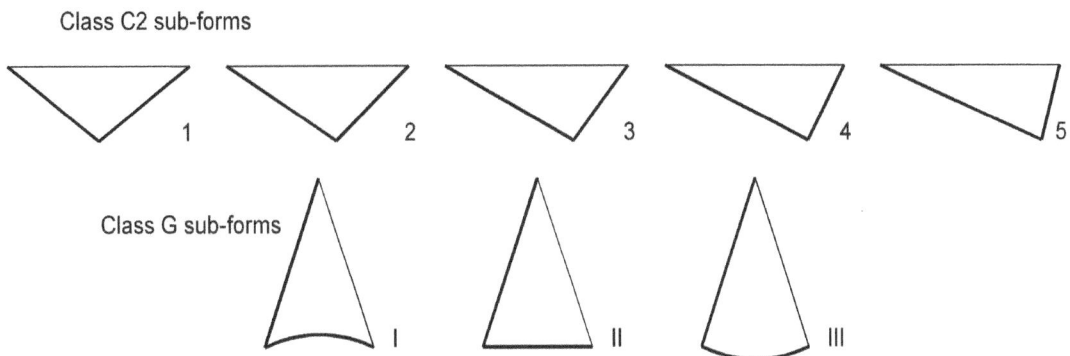

Panel 1, Fig. 2. Sub-forms of Classes C2 and G, identified in connection with the examination of the finds from Airhouse/Overhowden and other Late Neolithic Scottish assemblages. Thick lines represent edges characterized by continuous retouch.

dark-brown pieces (35%). In both cases, other flint forms are relatively rare (5-8%).

As shown in Table 4, the flints belong to two main types, namely a largely marbled grey flint and a more or less homogeneous dark-brown flint. The greys are slightly more varied than the dark-browns, and they grade from marbled (75%), through small-dotted (21%) to homogeneous (4%). Approximately three-quarters of the dark-browns are homogeneous, with one-fifth being marbled. The small-dotted variety corresponds almost exactly to the Juttish ('småprikket') flint described by Becker (1952, 77) in his discussion of the Middle to Late Neolithic 'trade' in flint from northern Jutland to southern Norway. It is thought that the British grey and dark-brown flint forms both date to roughly the same geological age as the flint quarried from Juttish mines in the later half of the Neolithic period. Although some coastal flint from Scotland (for example from Islay) may date to earlier parts of the Cretaceous period, such as the Campanian, most of the grey and dark-brown flints probably date (like the Juttish flint) to the Maastrichtian stage of the Cretaceous period (Harding *et al.* 2004, 87).

As suggested by Mulholland (1970; 85), probably mainly by applying 'Occam's Razor', the flints from Airhouse and Overhowden may mainly have been procured through exchange with groups in Yorkshire – the closest place from which this form of high-grade flint could have been procured. During a field-trip to flint sources in Yorkshire, local archaeologists Terry Manby and Peter Makey kindly showed the author a number of Yorkshire flint forms which, in terms of colours and patterning, corresponded almost exactly to the flints recovered from the two sites in the Scottish Borders, and the proposed link between Late Neolithic sites in south-east Scotland and the Yorkshire flint sources seems a likely one.

The Late Neolithic importation of flint into Scotland from primary sources is also supported by the fact that approximately 3% of the flint artefacts from Airhouse and Overhowden has surviving soft cortex. However, some of the darkest dark-brown flints, which appear almost black, resemble flint forms from south-east England closely, such as the forms exploited by the much later Brandon gunflint industry (Kenmotsu 1990, 95), and – although the author finds this unlikely – it cannot be ruled out that individual pieces in the Airhouse/Overhowden collection may have come from further afield than Yorkshire. High-grade flint may also be found in parts of Lincolnshire (Wilson 1948, 53), although not in the same amounts, and usually not in the form of equally large prime-quality nodules, as in Yorkshire. It is therefore necessary to emphasize that, when the term Yorkshire flint is used in the following text, this refers to flint from the 'greater Yorkshire area'.

Durden (1995, 410) distinguishes between two main sources of Yorkshire flint, namely flint from the Yorkshire Wolds and flint from the glacial till. The Wolds possess two sources of flint, namely primary flint from the chalk (as tabular flint in continuous beds, as well as bands of nodules) and derived nodular material. The former is very brittle, and the hardness of the chalk did not allow this resource to be mined. The derived flint, on the other hand, is known to have been exploited in prehistoric times. The till flint is available from a band along the east-coast, and it is of high quality.

The flint from the Wolds is mainly grey to white, whereas the till flint is mainly mottled to translucent grey, dark-brown or black, although small amounts of pink and reddish colours also occur. During his field-trip with Terry Manby, the author collected grey and dark-brown flint from the coast at Hornsea and, later, Manby kindly provided additional samples collected further to the south, from the coast at Withernsea. It is possible to collect the same types of flint at Flamborough Head towards the north (Henson 1982; Durden 1995, 410), with '*boulder clay sourced flint on the beaches north of Flamborough Head [being] smaller in size than south of Flamborough*' (Terry Manby pers. comm.). The vast majority of the Yorkshire flint dates to the Middle and Upper Chalk sequences of the Upper Cretaceous (Wilson 1948, 67-69), but some of the flint from the Wolds may date to the Lower Chalk sequence (Terry Manby pers. comm.). '*There are in the boulder clay [...] unrolled blocks of flint with sharp edges, retaining chalk cortex, [which] the glacier must have taken straight off outcropping strata on the bed of the North Sea*' (Manby in email to the author; 2009).

The chert artefacts from Airhouse and Overhowden are mainly in grey (58%) or black (27%) nuances, supplemented by small amounts of green (6%), brown (6%), and dark-blue (3%) chert. It is mainly homogeneous, or dotted/banded radiolarian chert, which may have been procured locally by the prehistoric quarrying of primary sources (Warren 2007, 147 [Wadd&Ped]), or it was possibly collected from derived pebble sources (Ballin 1999c, 82). The three pitchstone artefacts are in black aphyric material. Although, in Argyll & Bute, pitchstone may have been procured from the Isle of Arran through the Neolithic period and well into the Early Bronze Age, it is mostly associated with an extensive Early Neolithic exchange network.

Lithic raw materials as a diagnostic element is discussed further in Chapter 2.5.

2.3   Typological characterisation

In terms of lithic tool typology, the Late Neolithic period is a highly distinctive entity. However, not all the types referred to in the archaeological literature are equally well-defined (eg, some knife forms), and some rare types may not have been discussed at all (eg, certain polished-edge implements). The purpose of the present chapter is therefore, first, to define the main Late Neolithic tool types, as they are used in this paper, and, then, to characterize the individual lithic tool types recovered from the Airhouse and Overhowden sites.

2.3.1. Arrowheads

Petit tranchet derivative arrowheads

The most significant Late Neolithic artefact category is composed of the so-called *Petit tranchet* derivative arrowheads or, in short, PTDs, which in the present report has been chosen as the main diagnostic Late Neolithic artefact type. These pieces were introduced shortly after the beginning of the Impressed Ware period and they remained in use through this period and the succeeding Grooved Ware period (for period definitions, see Chapter 1.4). A detailed PTD typology was introduced by Clark (1934b), and it is still widely used today. As Green writes (1980, 30): '*Clark recognized that there was no sharp division between his types, which he lettered A to I, but he considered that the sub-divisions were necessary for the definition of the range of variation present within this class of artefacts*'.

Clark (1934b, 33; this volume's Panel 1) suggested to subdivide the arrowheads A to I into three formal groups, namely A, B-F, and G-I, where A is the archetypal (Mesolithic) *petit tranchet* arrowhead, '*antedating the whole group in its origin*'. Classes B-F, he claimed, appear to be directly descended from Class A, whereas Classes G-I represent '*alternative or divergent*' developments from the main group. However, he also suggests a functional subdivision of the Late Neolithic arrowheads, where the

morphological similarities between Classes B-C and the parent form, Class A, indicate that these more or less symmetrical pieces were hafted as transverse arrowheads, whereas the asymmetry of Classes D-I indicates that those were hafted obliquely, that is, with an acutely pointed tip, one sharp lateral cutting-edge, and one lateral barb. The interpretation of some pieces as transverse and some as pointed arrowheads is supported by macroscopic use-wear and breakage patterns (for example the pieces in the Airhouse/Overhowden collection).

Today, it is common to subdivide the Late Neolithic PTDs into two main groups, namely Classes B-D (transverse, or chisel-shaped, arrowheads; Fig. 4), and Classes E-I (oblique arrowheads; Fig. 5) (eg, Green 1980, 37; Butler 2005, 158). However, this subdivision is based largely on *subjective* impressions of arrowhead symmetry, as well as on the arrowheads' length:width ratio. Green chose to focus primarily on the two main dimensions of the PTDs, and he produced a diagram which supports this dichotomy (Green 1980, Fig. 15:upper). Unfortunately, he may have 'thrown the baby out with the bath water', as the inclusion of other variables (eg, the present paper) suggests a slightly more complex picture. The analysis of the arrowheads from Airhouse and Overhowden demonstrated that useful variables in the formal/functional grouping of PTDs are: 1) the length:width ratio; 2) the relative asymmetry; and 3) the relative concavity (the metric variables relevant to the characterization of British PTDs are explained in Fig. 2).

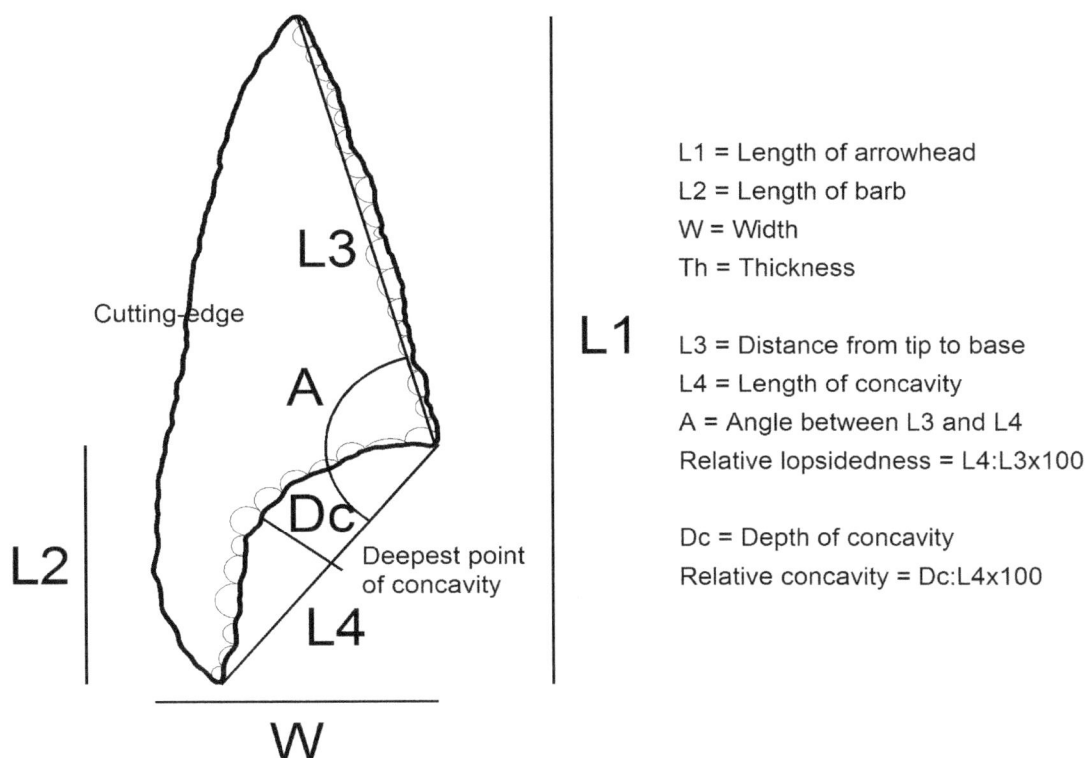

L1 = Length of arrowhead
L2 = Length of barb
W = Width
Th = Thickness

L3 = Distance from tip to base
L4 = Length of concavity
A = Angle between L3 and L4
Relative lopsidedness = L4:L3x100

Dc = Depth of concavity
Relative concavity = Dc:L4x100

Fig. 2. The metric variables of British PTDs.

Other metric variables may be equally useful, but as they basically describe the same formal variation as the above three variables, they were excluded from the present analysis. The South Scandinavian Kongemosian arrowheads, for example, undergo the same changes as the British Late Neolithic arrowheads (but instead of developing from transverse to pointed pieces, they developed from pointed to transverse pieces), and in his analysis of this metamorphosis Edinborough (2005, 54) used the angle (A) between the two modified edges (L3 and L4) to describe the phenomenon. Variation of this angle essentially describes development either from symmetrical pieces to asymmetrical pieces, or *vice versa* (ie, point 2 above: relative asymmetry).

The formal analysis of the lithic assemblages from Airhouse and Overhowden proved that not all Late Neolithic arrowheads fitted Clark's classes equally well (for detailed definitions of those, see Panel 1), and it was necessary to adapt his classification system to the specific case. He defined two sub-types of Class C, C1 and C2, where the former has a relatively short cutting-edge and the latter a longer cutting-edge. In his illustrations, both are represented by symmetrical pieces, whereas the C2 specimens recovered from Airhouse and Overhowden are mostly asymmetrical (Fig. 8) – some of those only differ from Class G specimens by having a straight shortest side, where Class G arrowheads may have a straight, slightly concave or slightly convex shortest side.

A number of hybrid forms were also defined, and when it was attempted to illustrate the formal variation of the Airhouse and Overhowden PTDs diagrammatically, small numerical categories occasionally had to be combined. The following groups were used:

- B/C1+B/D
- C1
- C1/D
- D
- C1/C2
- C2
- E
- F
- F/G+F/H
- G
- G/H+G/I
- H

Table 5. Formal groups used to sequence/group the PTDs from Airhouse and Overhowden

It was attempted to manipulate (sequence or group) these types in a way that would produce diagrammatical expressions which appeared logical (that is, non-random), with the diagrams focusing on the three variables listed above, or flint types (below). All other sequences than the one presented in Table 5 resulted in diagrammatical expressions which appeared random in one or all cases. It is therefore suggested that this sequence may represent some form of prehistoric reality, either formal evolution (ie, chronology), functional specialization or both. This problem needs further attention.

The suggestion that chronology may play a role in the formation of this sequence is backed by other assemblages and variations in the relative amounts of Impressed and Grooved Ware pottery (Chapter 1.4), which supports the formation of two basic groups, namely chisel-shaped and oblique arrowheads (as proposed by Green 1980, 37). It should, however, be borne in mind that some chisel-

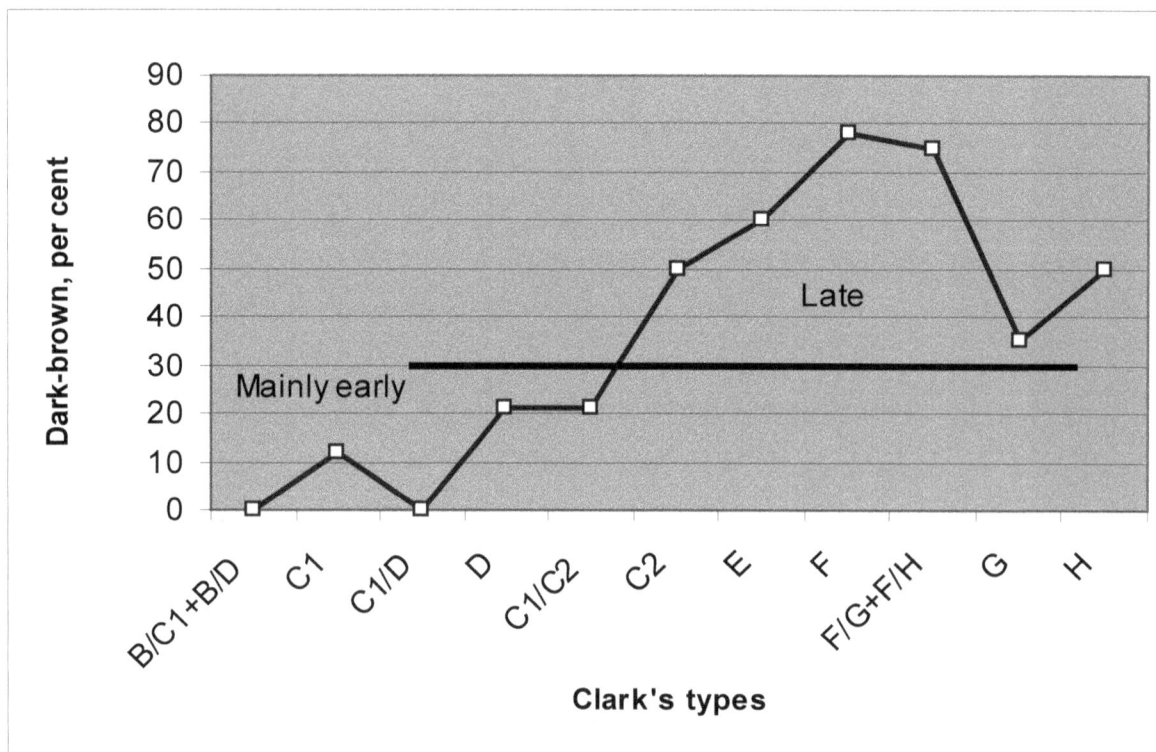

Fig. 3. The Airhouse/Overhowden PTD classes sequenced according to basic flint types (dark-brown pieces as a percentage of dark-brown+grey pieces).

shaped arrowheads have been found with oblique pieces (as at Storey's Bar Road, Pit W17; Pryor 1978, 104-5), and that chronology therefore cannot be the only answer.

When the author examined the arrowheads from Airhouse and Overhowden, it was noticed that there was a clear difference between the flint types used to manufacture the two main arrowhead types, and an attempt was made to quantify this observation (Fig. 3).

Classes B, C1, and D are characterized by less than 30% dark-brown flint, whereas Classes C2, E, F, G and H are characterized by more than 30% dark-brown flint (apart from Class G, more than 50% of the latter classes are in dark-brown flint; Class G may form part of a deviating functional or chronological group, and it is discussed further below). The definition of the two types, chisel-shaped and oblique arrowheads, as mainly early and late entities is based on the two types' association with Impressed Ware and Grooved Ware pottery (Chapter 1.4). The reality of these two basic types is supported by the average length:width ratios of the various arrowhead classes (Fig. 6), forming two clusters, an early cluster and a late one. This becomes clearer when it is proposed that the hybrid grouping C1/C2 may be an 'unnatural' construction, combining early (C1) and late (C2) elements, as well as, possibly, pieces with different functions (C1s may be transverse arrowheads and asymmetrical C2s pointed arrowheads; this is discussed further below).

If a diagram is produced, which is based on the average relative widths (W/L1x100) of the various classes (Fig. 7)[1], a regularly descending curve appears, indicating a potential (or mainly) chronological/evolutionary process. It is suggested that early PTDs (most chisel-shaped arrowheads) have average relative widths >70, whereas later PTDs (oblique arrowheads) have average relative widths <70. Only the hybrid grouping G/H+G/I does not fit well into the sequence and, as in the case of the C1/C2 grouping in Fig. 6, this may be due to the 'unnatural' combination of arrowheads with different dates or functions (Class G and Classes H+I).

A diagram (Fig. 8) showing the various classes' average relative asymmetry (L4/L3x100) produces a similar curve, and in this case a group of mainly early PTDs are defined by an average relative asymmetry >80 (the higher the ratio, the more symmetrical the piece), whereas assumedly later pieces are defined by an average relative asymmetry <80. In Fig. 8, Class C2 and the Grouping G/H+G/I appear out of place and, possibly, for the same reason as classes or groupings formed deviations from the trends in Figs 2.3.1-2-4.

Finally, the various classes of PTDs were positioned in relation to each other on the basis of their average relative

_____

[1] If PTDs were only slightly damaged, original dimensions were estimated on the basis of the truncated dimensions.

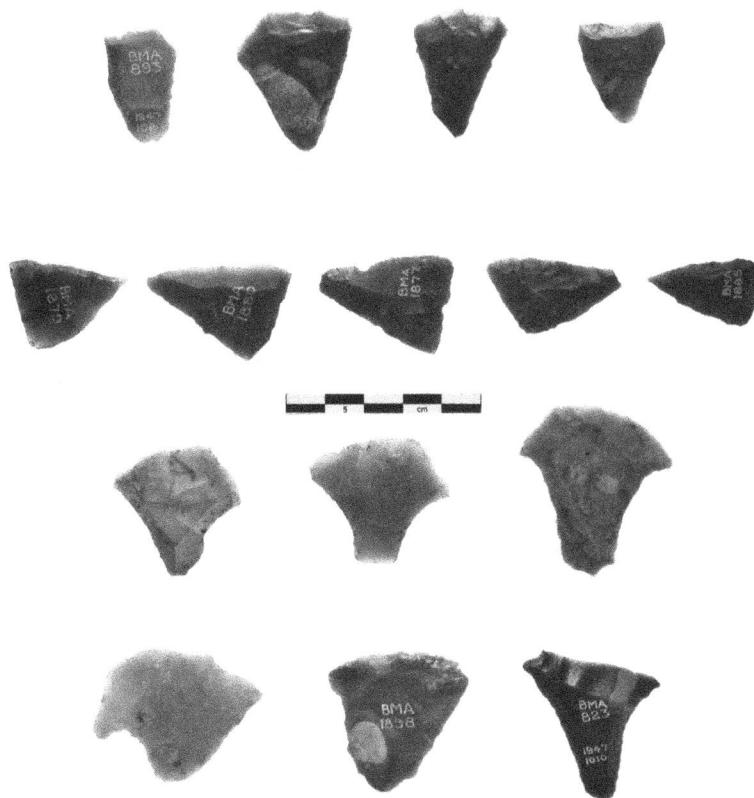

Fig. 4. Chisel-shaped arrowheads from Overhowden and Airhouse, Classes B1/C1 (BMA 893), C1 (BMA 537, 136, 137), C1/C2 (BMA 1879, 1880), C2 (BMA 1877, 266, 1885) C1/D (BMA 135, 133, 123), and D (720, 1898, 823).

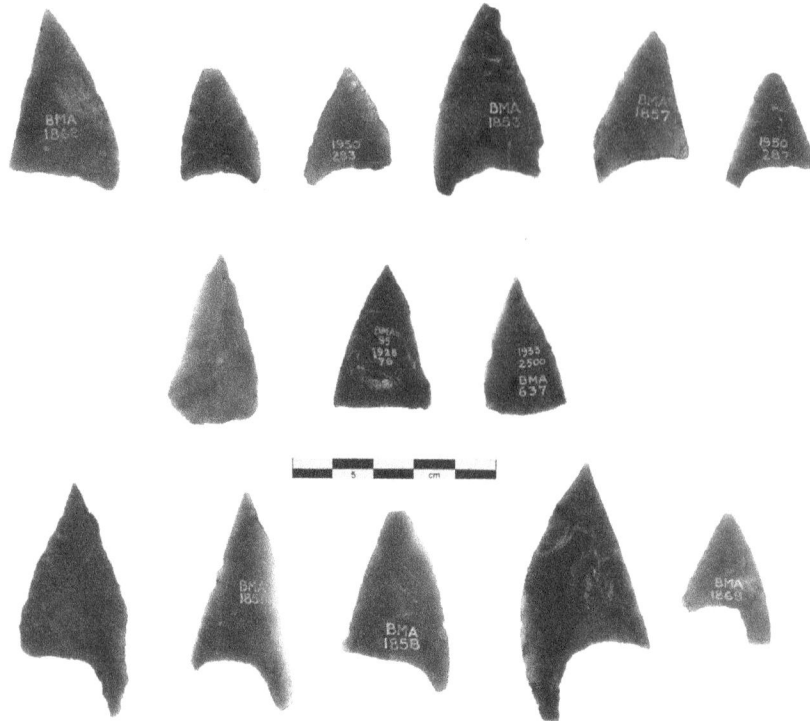

Fig. 5. Oblique arrowheads from Overhowden and Airhouse, Classes E (BMA 1862, 92, 1866), F (BMA 1853, 1857, 1870), G (BMA 539, 95, 637), H (BMA 87, 1851, 1858), I (BMA 86), and H/I (BMA 1869).

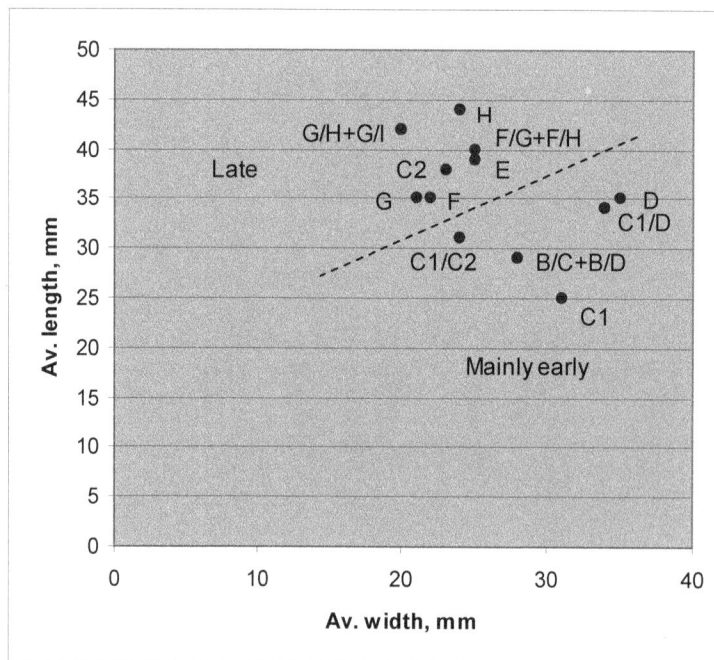

Fig. 6. The Airhouse/Overhowden PTD classes positioned in relation to each other according to their average length:width ratios.

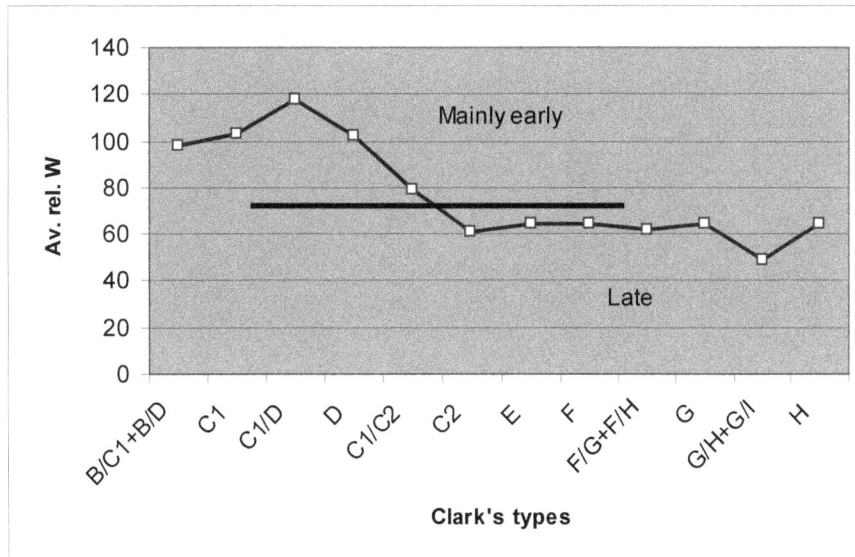

Fig. 7. The Airhouse/Overhowden PTD classes positioned in relation to each other according to their average relative widths.

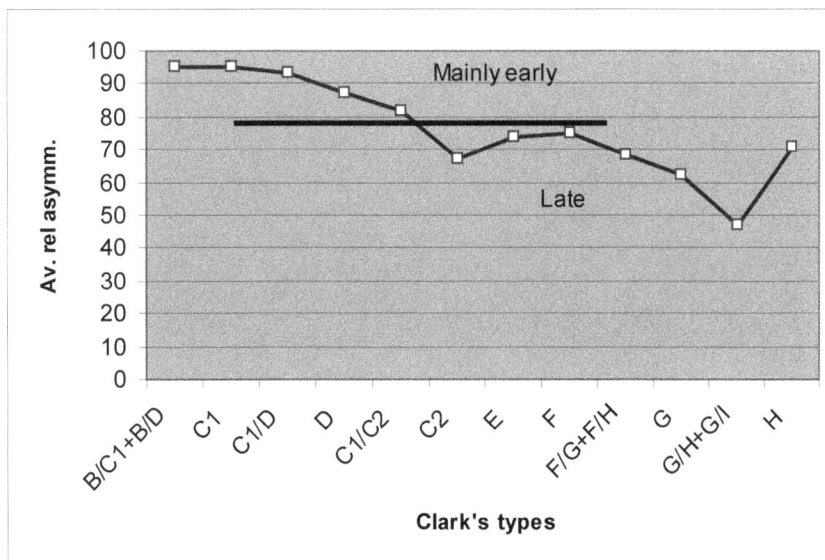

Fig. 8. The Airhouse/Overhowden PTD classes positioned in relation to each other according to their average relative asymmetry.

concavities (Dc/L4x100), resulting in the curve displayed in Fig. 9. This curve is more fluctuating than those of the previous diagrams (Figs 6-8), but the general trend is that mostly early PTDs have average relative concavities <5 (weakly developed concavities) and later PTDs >5 (distinct concavities). In this case the later group (ie, pieces with marked concavities) includes Class D, whereas the earlier group (ie, pieces without concavities, or with poorly developed concavities) only embrace Classes B and C1. The classes/groupings C1/C2, C2, G, and G/H+G/I deviate from the general trend by having no or poorly developed concavities.

In most respects, Fig. 3, and Figs 6-9 support the distinction between largely early chisel-shaped pieces and late oblique arrowheads, as proposed by Clark (1934b)

and Green (1980). However, there are obvious problems associated with fitting the Classes C2 (asymmetrical) and G into any general trends, and these problems also concern groupings of arrowheads which include these two classes (eg, C1/C2 and G/H+G/I). These two classes (C2 and G) are defined by: 1) low to medium ratios of dark-brown flint; 2) low average relative width; 3) low to medium average relative asymmetry ratios; and 4) weakly developed lateral concavities. The trends of the now three groups are summarized in Table 6.

The general association of chisel-shaped pieces with Impressed Ware (although, as mentioned above, some chisel-shaped pieces have been found with oblique arrowheads) and oblique arrowheads with Grooved Ware indicates that the two groups do represent mainly early

17

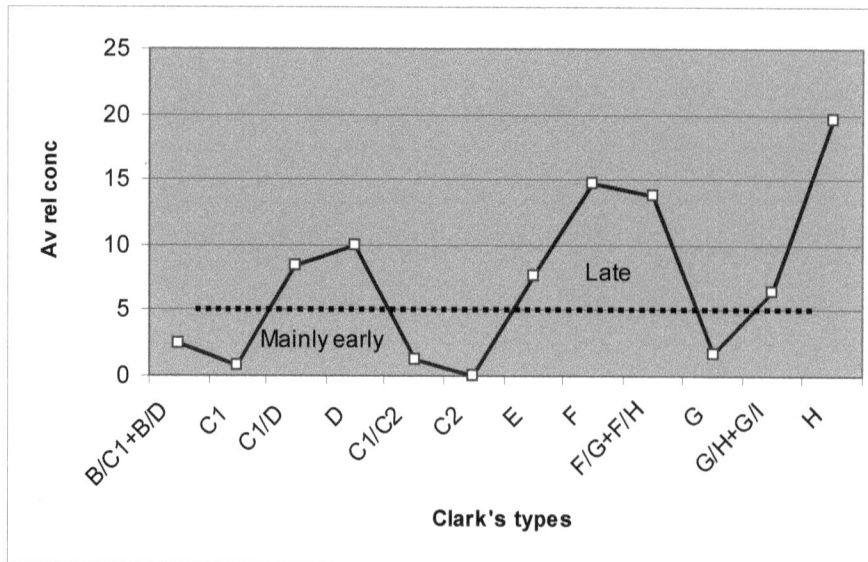

Fig. 9. The Airhouse/Overhowden PTD classes positioned in relation to each other according to their average relative concavities.

	Chisel-shaped pieces (B/C1/D)	Deviating group (C2/G)	Oblique pieces (E/F/H/I)
Dark-brown flint ratios	Low (0-30)	Low-medium (35-50)	High (50-80)
Average relative width	High (>80)	Low-medium (50-60)	Medium (65)
Average relative asymmetry ratios	High (80-95)	Low (45-70)	Medium (70-75)
Developed lateral concavities	Low (0-3) [B-C1]	Low (0-3) [C2/G]	High (7-20) [D/E/F/H/I]

Table 6. The three proposed formal groups of PTDs.

as well as late arrowhead types. The sliding character of (particularly the first half of) the produced curves supports Clark's suggestion that the more developed forms may represent evolution of earlier, less developed forms (above).

However, this is probably only a partial picture: although a gradual evolution may have taken place, for example transforming larger early pieces into slimmer and more gracile later forms, the introduction of a new functional principle (acutely pointed arrowheads) must have been relatively abrupt. This is suggested by the use-wear of the two groups, where the edges of typical chisel-shaped pieces indicate hafting of those as transverse arrowheads (chipped transverse edges), whereas the damaged or broken-off points of oblique pieces indicate hafting of those as arrowheads with acutely pointed tips. In a sense, this corresponds to being pregnant – you cannot be 'a bit pregnant', you either are or you are not; in this case, the pieces were either hafted as transverse or tipped pieces.

The finds from Pit W17 at Fengate (Pryor 1978, 104-5), where chisel-shaped and oblique arrowheads were recovered together, suggest the following chronological scenario: 1) chisel-shaped arrowheads were introduced early in the Impressed Ware period; 2) then, oblique arrowheads were introduced at the beginning of the Grooved Ware period, and the two types and functions co-

existed for a time (Pit W17); and 3) finally, chisel-shaped arrowheads were phased out and oblique arrowheads reigned supreme. The latter stage is still somewhat hypothetical (although see Wainwright & Longworth 1971, Fig. 95; Healy 1985, Table 10), and it may be confirmed/rejected by analysis of the many PTDs from Durrington Walls (Chan forthcoming).

It is difficult to fit arrowheads of Classes C2 (where the C2 points from Airhouse and Overhowden belong to a clearly asymmetrical variety [Fig. 8], primarily differing from Class G by their simpler modification and the non-concave delineation of the shorter retouched edge) and G into this general development. Classes C2 and G's relatively high ratio of grey flint suggests that these pieces may be relatively early, and they may form an intermediary chronological group between chisel-shaped and oblique arrowheads (although use-wear, such as broken-off tips, indicate a close functional relationship with the later group). The fact that several arrowheads of Class G have full bifacial retouch supports the suggestion that these pieces belong to the later group of more accomplished arrowheads. However, allowing asymmetrical C2 points and G points to form an intermediary group creates a new problem, namely how to fit pieces of Class D into any sequence, as the distinct lateral concavities of these pieces indicate that Class D arrowheads are relatively late in the sequence, whereas Class C2 and G arrowheads are characterized by having weakly developed lateral concavities.

The presently available evidence does not provide any definitive answers to these questions, and it is suggested, for the time being, simply to accept that three formal groups exist, namely 1) chisel-shaped arrowheads (Classes B, C1, symmetrical C2s, and D); 2) arrowheads belonging to a deviating group (asymmetrical C2s and Class G); and 3) oblique arrowheads (Classes E, F, H, and I). The chisel-shaped pieces were hafted as transverse arrowheads, and pieces belonging to the other two groups were (as suggested by use-wear and breakage patterns) hafted as acutely pointed arrowheads.

To reach a fuller understanding of how these pieces relate to each other, in an evolutionary sense as well as in a functional sense, it is necessary to analyse arrowheads from well-dated Late Neolithic single-occupation sites (where Airhouse and Overhowden both represent activities over a prolonged period), as well as to carry out proper use-wear analysis of the arrowheads by the application of high-powered magnification. It should not be ruled out that some of Clark's classes could be contemporaneous and, for example, related to events of higher and lower status (eg, more or less well-executed pieces; pieces with 'ordinary' barbs and exaggerated barbs; pieces with unifacial and bifacial invasive retouch).

It should be emphasized that, due to the fact that Clark's classes are not metrically or morphologically well-defined, many borderline cases exist. It is particularly difficult to distinguish between the two deviating types, C2 and G (see Panel 1).

Following the proposed PTD definitions and groupings, the Late Neolithic arrowheads from the two sites may be quantified as in Table 7. The Airhouse site is clearly dominated by chisel-shaped arrowheads (57%), whereas the Overhowden site is dominated by oblique arrowheads and arrowheads of the deviating group (70%). Twenty pieces with bifacial retouch of both faces were recovered; in nine of these cases, the bifacial retouch also covers the cutting-edge. All bifacial PTDs belong to either the deviating group or the oblique arrowheads (Classes C2/G and E/F/H/I). The bifacial pieces are distributed evenly across the Airhouse and Overhowden assemblages. Four pieces (BMA 88, 89, 1854, 1867) – two from each site – were defined as ripple-flaked, that is, with fine parallel removals covering most of one or both faces. All ripple-flaked pieces belong to Class H. Five rough-outs – that is, unfinished pieces – were excluded from the typological discussion (above), as were 26 atypical or unclassifiable (heavily fragmented) specimens. Only one piece is burnt (BMA 265).

Fig. 6, which formed part of the discussion of the PTD typology, gives a visual impression of the average sizes of the individual PTD variants. The exact average dimensions of the PTD variants from Airhouse/Overhowden are given in Table 8. These data are then summarized by main category in Table 9. Fig. 2 gives an overview of the metric variables of the British PTDs.

	Quantity			Per cent		
	Airhouse	*Overhowden*	*Total*	*Airhouse*	*Overhowden*	*Total*
Chisel-shaped arrowheads	105	14	119	57	24	49
Deviating group	37	20	57	20	35	24
Oblique arrowheads	15	20	35	8	35	14
Rough-outs	4	1	5	2	1	2
Unclassifiable/atypical	23	3	26	13	5	11
TOTAL	**184**	**58**	**242**	**100**	**100**	**100**

Table 7. Typological list of the PTDs from Airhouse and Overhowden.

PTD variants	Length	Width	Thickness
B/C1+B/D	29	28	4.3
C1	25	31	4.5
C1/C2	31	24	4.4
C1/D	34	34	4.5
D	35	35	4.9
C2	38	23	5.3
E	39	25	4.6
F	35	22	4.2
F/G+F/H	40	25	5.0
G	35	21	4.7
G/H+G/I	42	20	5.4
H	44	24	5.0

Table. 8. The average dimensions of the individual PTD variants (mm).

	Length	Width	Thickness
Chisel-shaped arrowheads	25-35	24-35	4.3-4.9
Deviating types	35-38	21-23	4.7-5.3
Oblique arrowheads	35-44	22-25	4.2-4.7

Table. 9. The average dimensions of the main PTD categories (mm).

	Quantity			Per cent		
	Airhouse	*Overhowden*	*Total*	*Airhouse*	*Over-howden*	*Total*
Leaf-shaped arrowheads	31	4	35	13	6	11
Petit tranchet derivative arrowheads	184	58	242	78	85	80
Barbed-and-tanged arrowheads	20	6	26	9	9	9
TOTAL	**235**	**68**	**303**	**100**	**100**	**100**

Table 10. Relative numbers of main arrowhead types by site.

Five PTDs are positively based on Levallois-like flakes (BMA 263, 274, 281.34, 540, 876). However, it is thought that practically all PTDs may be formed on Levallois-like blanks, but that – due to extensive edge and invasive retouch – most of those blanks cannot be identified as such.

Early Neolithic and Early Bronze Age arrowheads

Arrowheads pre- or post-dating the Late Neolithic period include Early Neolithic leaf-shaped pieces and Early Bronze Age barbed-and-tanged pieces. As shown in Table 10, PTDs outnumber other arrowheads by a ratio of four to one (80%). Leaf-shaped and barbed-and-tanged pieces are roughly equally common (11% and 9%, respectively).

As mentioned in the paper's raw material chapter (Chapter 2.2), the leaf-shaped and barbed-and-tanged arrowheads include considerably higher proportions of non-flint than the PTDs. Only one PTD is in chert (c. 0.5%), whereas one-third (34%) of the leaf-shaped arrowheads are in this material, and one-tenth (11%) of the barbed-and-tanged arrowheads; one leaf-shaped point is in chalcedony (for a more detailed account of the cherts, see Chapter 2.2).

Approximately 15% of the Early Neolithic points are kite-shaped, whereas all Early Bronze Age points belong to the Sutton type. Kite-shaped arrowheads are generally considered later Early Neolithic pieces, and associated with the earlier part of the Impressed Ware period (Green 1980, 85; Clarke *et al.* 1985, 63-67). The fact that all barbed-and-tanged pieces belong to the Sutton type, and that for example no late Kilmarnock points (with triangular or pointed tangs) are present, may indicate that most of these pieces date to a relatively early part of the Early Bronze Age. Or to put it differently: the two collections' Early Neolithic arrowheads may not *pre*-date the Late Neolithic finds from Airhouse and Overhowden by much, and the Early Bronze Age arrowheads may not *post*-date those finds by much (also see Chapters 2.5 and 4.2).

Schemes for the characterization of leaf-shaped and barbed-and-tanged arrowheads were proposed by Green (1980),

and his systems are generally referred to when British Neolithic and Bronze Age arrowheads are characterized and discussed (eg, Butler 2005). Leaf-shaped arrowheads are usually subdivided along two axes, one of which defines an arrowhead's size (Classes 1-4; large to small), whereas the other axis defines an arrowhead's slenderness (Classes A-C; squat to slender). Approximately two-thirds (65%) of the leaf-shaped pieces from Airhouse and Overhowden are small, with c. one-quarter (25%) being slightly larger; only 10% of the arrowheads belong to the two largest classes, 1 and 2 (Fig. 10). The vast majority of the leaf-shaped pieces are squat (60%), with approximately one-quarter (25%) being of intermediate form, and less than one-fifth (15%) are slender. Two pieces are slightly ogival (BMA 535, 1899), and one is burnt (BMA 275).

Green's scheme for the characterization of barbed-and-tanged arrowheads includes some 'fancy' forms (ie, pieces with so-called 'shaped' barbs and/or tangs), and some more 'common' forms. None of the Early Bronze Age points from Airhouse and Overhowden are 'fancy' in this respect. It is possible to subdivide the 'common' forms into three subtypes, namely Sutton a-c. Sutton a points are generally characterized by having no or vestigial barbs; Sutton b points by having round or square barbs ('unshaped'); and Sutton c points by having pointed barbs. They all have fairly plain tangs, and they are all classed as small, that is, lighter than 8 grammes and shorter than 50 mm (Fig. 11). The Early Bronze Age arrowheads from Airhouse and Overhowden include 30% Sutton a points, 52% Sutton b points, and 17% Sutton c points. Although no actual 'fancy' types were recovered at Airhouse and Overhowden, two of the sites' Sutton b points are as well-executed as those (BMA 66, 1905). BMA 66, a Sutton a point, has an unusually long tang.

Most of the leaf-shaped and barbed-and-tanged arrowheads have full invasive retouch of both faces, but a small number of pieces were shaped by simple edge-retouch (eg, BMA 281.21), whereas several were manufactured by bifacial, semi-invasive retouch of edges, barbs and tangs (BMA 281.32-33).

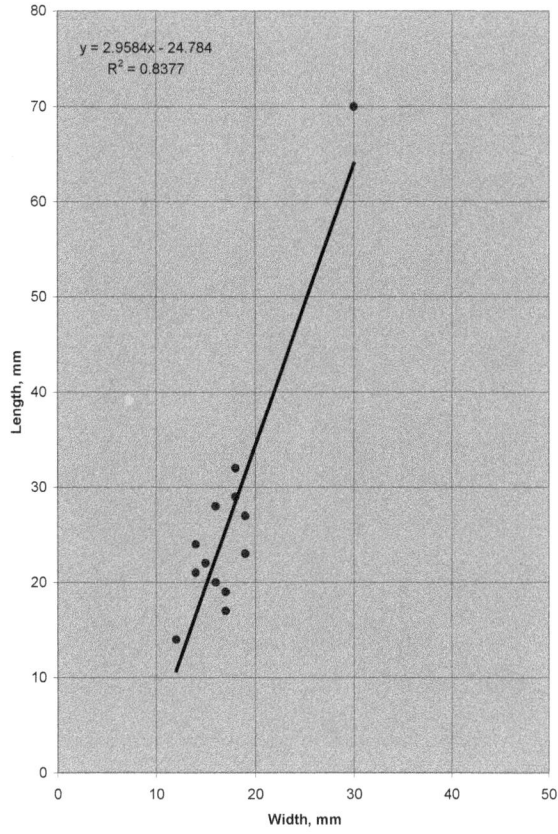

Fig. 10. The dimensions of all intact leaf-shaped arrowheads.

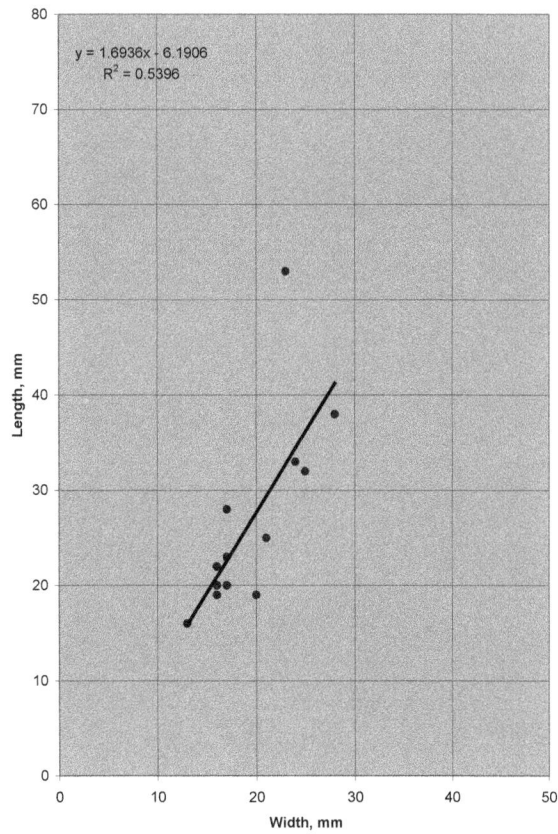

Fig. 11. The dimensions of all intact barbed-and-tanged arrowheads.

Fig. 12. Edge-polished adze-head from Airhouse (BMA 41).

2.3.2 Adzeheads

Only one axe- or adzehead was recovered from the two neighbouring sites (BMA 41; Airhouse; Fig. 12), and its asymmetrical cross-section defines it as an adzehead. The object is intact, and it measures 86 x 52 x 20 mm. It is in grey small-dotted flint, and it is characterized by impurities in the form of large internal chalk balls: one of those has been sectioned by the implement's left lateral side, one by its right lateral side, and one by its butt. One small pot-lid flake was detached from one face as a combined effect of internal impurities and frost-action. A thin 5-10 mm broad band along the working-edge, both faces, have been neatly polished, but no other parts of the adzehead's two faces were modified in this manner. Both faces were shaped by detaching thin flakes from two lateral knapping seams, running from cutting-edge to butt. These attributes define the piece as a two-sided, edge-polished adzehead. The two lateral sides are straight, but diverging towards the edge. In this respect, the present adzehead differs from the typical Late Neolithic edge-polished axeheads/adzeheads of Seamer/Duggleby Type, with their characteristic concave lateral sides.

2.3.3 Knives

As shown in Table 2, the two assemblages include relatively high proportions of knives (7%). However, the group 'combined tools' also incorporates cutting implements, as all tools in this category are combinations of knives and either scrapers, piercers or strike-a-lights. This category makes up 3% of the total number of tools from Airhouse and Overhowden (dealt with in Chapter 2.3.8). Unfortunately not all knife forms are equally well

defined, and in the following text an attempt is made to define the various forms of cutting implements discovered during the examination of the Airhouse/Overhowden collection (apart from cutting implements with serrated edges; Chapter 2.3.7). This chapter deals with backed knives, scale-flaked knives, plano-convex knives, discoidal knives, and polished-edge knives.

Backed knives are the morphologically simplest cutting implements. In her report on the finds from the Wissey Embayment (The Fenland Project; Healy 1996, 76), as well as in her guidelines for the lithic analysis of the finds from the Raunds Project (Healy, unpublished notes), Healy defines the backed knife as: '*A generally parallel-sided blank, one lateral side of which is blunted by abrupt retouch, the opposite side being either unretouched, although often worn, or modified by uni- or bifacial flat retouch*'. In the present report, a backed knife is defined as '*a generally parallel-sided blank, one lateral side of which is blunted by abrupt retouch, the opposite side being unretouched*', as flat retouch of the cutting-edge would create an overlap with the definition of scale-flaked knives (below).

Plano-convex knives were discussed by Clark (1932a), but unfortunately he did not explain how these were to be clearly distinguished from their close formal relatives, the scale-flaked knives. As pointed out by Clark (ibid., 158), the term 'plano-convex knife' '*... accurately describes the section of the implement*', which was usually produced on an elongated flake or blade, and '*... the point is normally obtuse, if not rounded ...*'. It is easy to understand why the term 'slug-knife' was adopted by earlier generations of archaeologists for certain small Early Bronze Age knives, but this term should be avoided as not all plano-convex knives (and particularly not the Late Neolithic ones) are small and slug-shaped (cf. Clark 1932a, Pl. XXXII).

The important detail, when considering plano-convex knives against scale-flaked knives, is the point that their plano-convex shape must have been formed by invasive retouch, and not simply by the incidental shape of the original blank. Usually, their entire dorsal face is covered by invasive retouch, although on occasion small areas of untouched original surface remains along the top of the dorsal 'back' of the knife. In addition, their cutting-edge(s) may have been shaped by (usually partial) invasive retouch of the ventral face, although this is not a typological requirement.

In contrast, scale-flaked knives were shaped entirely by invasive retouch ('scale-flaking') of their cutting-edge(s), usually in association with abrupt retouch of the lateral side opposite the cutting-edge. This retouch may be dorsal, ventral or both. As noticed by Healy (1996, 76), the blanks of scale-flaked knives are usually parallel-sided flakes or blades. Where Plano-convex and scale-flaked knives tend to be associated with Late Neolithic and Early Bronze Age industries, backed knives may be found in most prehistoric contexts (eg, Butler 2005, 112, 129, 170).

Two knife forms are associated exclusively with the Late Neolithic period, namely discoidal knives and polished-edge knives. The former is a group of related knife forms, some of which may be of discoidal shape, but several of which are not. They were characterized by Clark (1932b), who suggested the following sub-forms:

I.   This form retains the general outline of the scraper, from which Clark (?erroneously) assumed they descended. These pieces may be semi-circular or circular.
II.   Triangular knives, which may be sub-divided into acutely-angled and obtusely-angled variants.
III. Lozenge-shaped or leaf-shaped knives.
IV.   Rectangular knives, which are frequently shaped like super-ellipsoids (Vestergård 2005). Most likely, the so-called Shetland knives (which are in felsite and not flint) represent exaggerated variants of this form (cf. Ballin forthcoming c).

Generally, the discoidal knives are based on flint flakes and shaped by a combination of bifacial flaking and grinding/polish of both faces.

The polished-edge knives were discussed by Manby (1974, 86) in his volume on the Grooved Ware sites of Yorkshire. They appear largely to have been based on regular elongated flakes or, more commonly, stout broad-blades. Following their level of sophistication, it is possible to subdivide these knives into three main forms, namely:

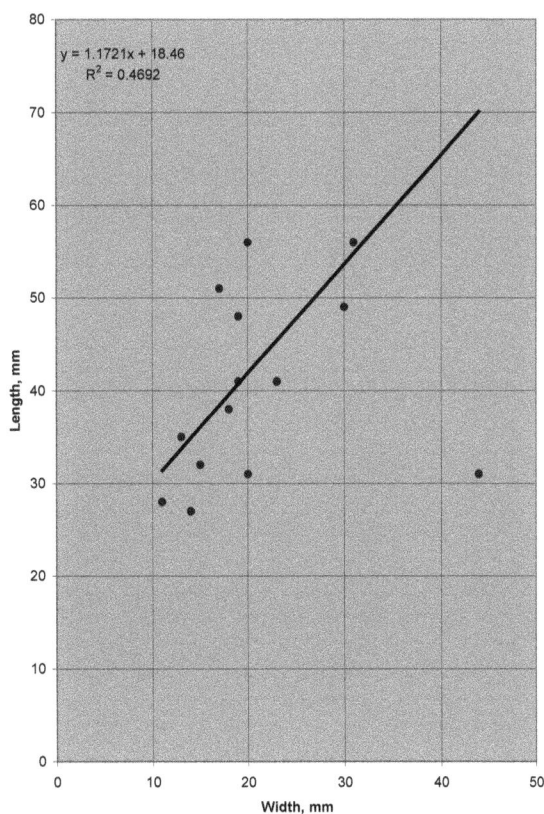

Fig. 13. The dimensions of all intact plano-convex (1) and scale-flaked (13) knives. The trendline and its correlation coefficient (R2) were calculated on the basis of all knives but the solitary outsider (31 x 44 mm).

1) Simple elongated flakes or blades with unifacial or bifacial polish of one or more edges and possibly parts of one or both faces (eg, ibid., Fig. 37.10, 12);
2) Well-executed scale-flaked or plano-convex knives with polished edges and, occasionally, parts of one or more faces (eg, ibid., Fig. 37.17, 18); and
3) Pieces with fully polished faces (eg, ibid., Fig. 36.1-7).

The polished-edge knives may be slightly earlier than the discoidal knives, with the former possible dating primarily to the Impressed Ware period, whereas the more sophisticated discoidal knives largely date to the Grooved Ware period (ibid., 86; also Butler 2005, 170).

Only one backed knife was recovered from the two sites (BMA 887). It is the medial-distal fragment of a flake knife (43 x 24 x 7 mm) with convex blunting along its right lateral side, and a slightly concave unmodified cutting-edge along the left lateral side.

With 35 pieces, scale-flaked knives are the most common knife form from Airhouse and Overhowden, two-thirds of which are based on blades and one-third on elongated flakes (Fig. 14). Seven pieces are based on Levallois-like blanks (BMA 5, 281.57, 281.71, 662, 857, 859, 884). Thirteen intact specimens have average dimensions of 40 x 21 x 7 mm (Fig. 13). Approximately two-thirds of the pieces have two opposed cutting-edges, whereas the remainder only have one. The single-edged pieces usually have steep blunting along the lateral side opposite the cutting-edge. The scale-flaked knives vary in terms of execution, with some being expedient (eg, BMA 281.72), whereas others (eg, BMA 768), due to their more complete cover of invasive retouch, are hybrid forms between scale-

flaked knives and plano-convex knives. One piece has a slightly serrated cutting-edge (BMA 106), and two are equipped with a hafting notch (BMA 773; 1919). Four pieces have had their bulbar area removed by flat retouch. Three pieces are burnt.

Four plano-convex knives are all blade-based (Fig. 14). The only intact piece measures 41 x 19 x 8 mm (Fig. 13). They are generally double-edged, and they have full dorsal retouch. One distal fragment has a convex termination, which was clearly not used for scraping (cf., Clark's characterization of this type; above).

Only one discoidal knife (BMA 795; Airhouse) and one polished-edge knife (BMA 1909; Overhowden) were recovered from the two sites (Fig. 15). The discoidal knife (58 x 49 x 13 mm) is of oval to rectangular shape (Type I/IV?), thinned by coarse invasive retouch. One edge has been sharpened by grinding/polish, which has also removed most of the dorsal cortex. The other three sides have been blunted. The polished-edge knife is the medial-distal fragment of a modified blade in yellow flint (44 x 17 x 6 mm). The left lateral side, dorsal face, as well as the entire ventral face, has been polished to provide a sharp cutting-edge. It has additional fine retouch of the right lateral side (Type 1).

Six scale-flaked knives (BMA 281.66, 655, 723, 769, 859, 860) display obvious gloss (Juel Jensen 1994, 20) along one or more edges, and, occasionally, these pieces also have gloss on parts of their ventral faces or dorsal ridges. Three of these (BMA 281.66, 655, 769) were presented to use-wear specialist Dr Randy Donahue, University of Bradford, who carried out a cursory examination of the specimens. His verdict was the same in all three cases,

Fig. 14. Scale-flaked and plano-convex knives from Overhowden and Airhouse (BMA 1911, 711, 106, 859, 768, 767).

Fig. 15. Polished-edge knife (BMA 1909) and discoidal knife(BMA 795) from Overhowden and Airhouse, respectively.

namely that the knives had been used for cutting/sickling grasses or cereals.

Single-piece curved sickles were discussed by Clark (1934a), and his distribution map (ibid., 75) shows that practically all known curved flint sickles have been found along the east-coast of England, from the English Channel to Yorkshire. One solitary piece has been found north of Yorkshire, near Balveny Castle in Banff (Mitchell 1889, 18). Most likely, the Scottish scale-flaked and plano-convex knives are also sickles, and they probably carried out the same work as the curved sickles of southern Britain.

2.3.4 Scrapers

The scrapers from Airhouse and Overhowden may be characterized by reference to standard scraper typologies (eg, Clark 1960; Butler 2005, 166). The relevant types are:

1) Discoidal scrapers;
2) Short end-scrapers;
3) Blade-scrapers;
4) Double-scrapers (ie, double end-scrapers);
5) Side-scrapers;
6) Side-/end-scrapers;
7) Concave scrapers; and
8) Indeterminate scraper-edge fragments.

All of these forms may, in addition to their modified working-edges, have modification in the form of blunting. This occasionally creates new scraper types, such as the popularly termed horseshoe-scraper, which is a short end-scraper with full (or almost full) bilateral blunting. Discoidal scrapers, which are round scrapers with working-edges that cover their entire, or most of their circumference,

are frequently very small. These small discoidal scrapers are generally referred to as button-scrapers or thumbnail-scrapers. In connection with his characterization of the lithic assemblage from the Early Bronze Age site of Dalmore on Lewis, the author suggested that thumbnail-scrapers from the Scottish Western Isles and the Scottish west-coast are defined as such if they have a maximum diameter of 23 mm (Ballin 2002b), but that they may be slightly larger in parts of Scotland and southern Britain where flint supplies are more plentiful. For an overview of the scraper types retrieved at Airhouse and Overhowden, see Table 1. Most prehistoric scrapers have steep scraper-edges, but approximately one-quarter of the Airhouse/ Overhowden scraper collection has acute, or relatively acute working-edges. Practically all scrapers from the two sites show clear macroscopic signs of having been used.

The two sites yielded eight discoidal scrapers, seven of which are based on flakes, with one (BMA 787) being based on a small chunk. Six intact pieces have average dimensions of 26 x 24 x 8 mm, suggesting that these small scrapers are somewhat larger in the Scottish Borders (where flint is relatively plentiful due to the importation of raw material from Yorkshire) than in the west of Scotland (where flint is a rare commodity). In one case (BMA 172), the bulb-of-percussion was removed by flat ventral retouch. One (BMA 1939) may be a small double-scraper, where the two opposed terminal working-edges are joined by lateral blunting, rather than a true discoidal scraper with a working-edge running along the entire circumference.

In total, 113 short end-scrapers were collected (Fig. 16). The vast majority of those are based on flakes (106 pieces), with the remainder being on spent bipolar, Levallois-like

25

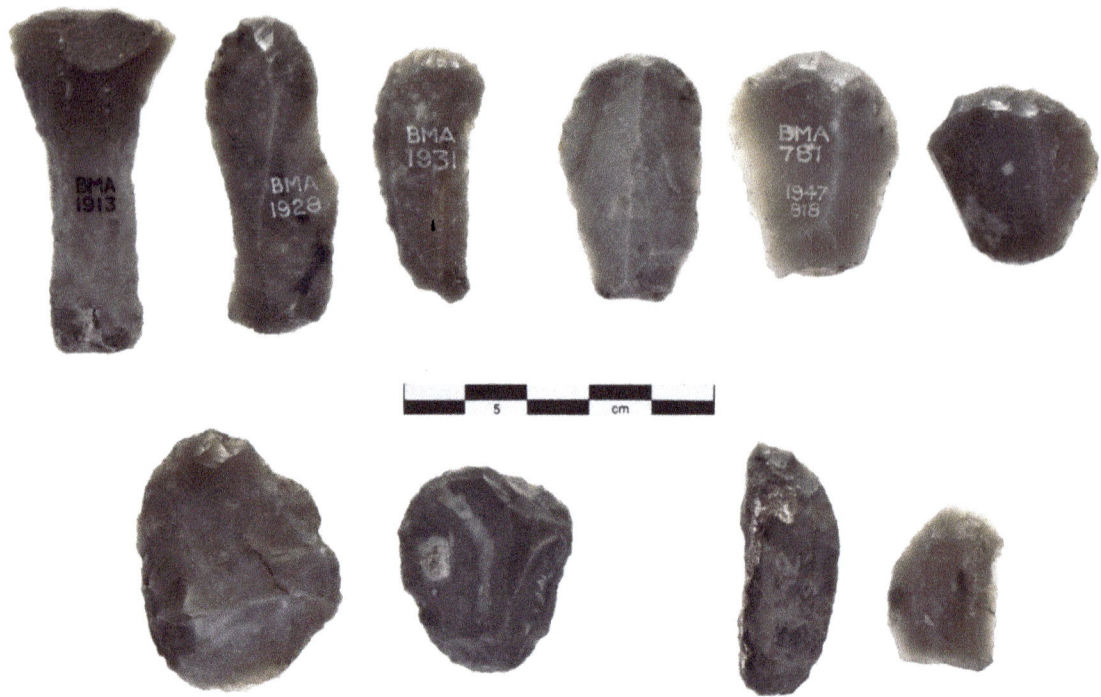

Fig. 16. Blade-scrapers (BMA 1913, 1928, 1931), short end-scrapers (BMA 253, 781, 194), double-scrapers (BMA 710, 181) and side-scrapers (BMA 161, 226) from Overhowden and Airhouse.

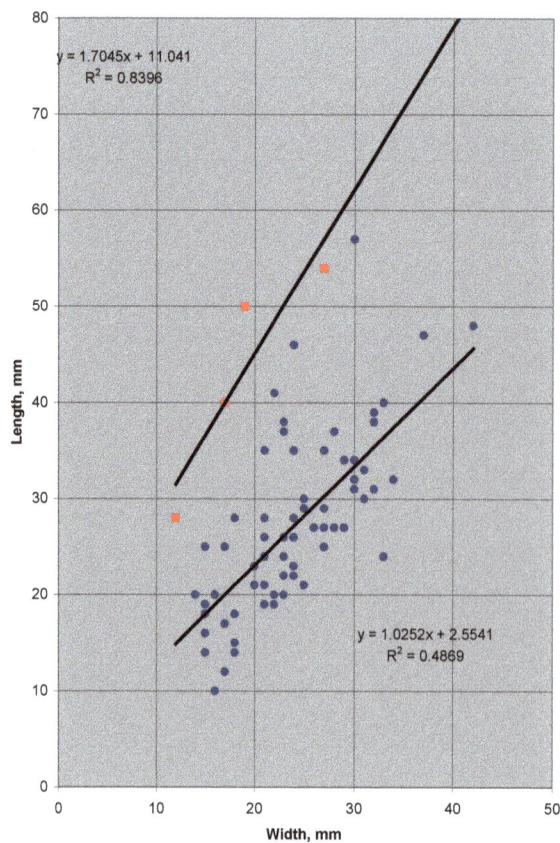

Fig. 17. The dimensions of all intact short end-scrapers (blue) and blade-scrapers (red).

or indeterminate cores. Sixteen of the flake blanks were struck from Levallois-like cores (BMA 171, 187, 194, 195, 212, 227, 235, 281.73, 349, 688, 699, 781, 836, 1932, 1933, 1938). They are generally fairly large, approximately oval scrapers, with average dimensions of 84 x 74 x 25 mm (Fig. 17). Nine pieces have proximal working-edges, with the remainder having distal working-edges. Roughly 40% of the latter have two fully blunted lateral sides, whereas the rest are without lateral blunting, or only one side is blunted. Three pieces have had their bulb-of-percussion removed by flat retouch. Nine pieces are burnt.

The Airhouse/Overhowden assemblage also embraces seven blade-scrapers (Fig. 16). Their assignation to the Late Neolithic bulk of the two assemblages is important, as it has been claimed by various analysts (Butler 2005, 166) that the production of blade-scrapers had seized by the onset of the Late Neolithic period. This claim is based on the erroneous assumption that blade production in general had seized by then (eg, the author; also Butler [2005, 157] who suggests that blades in Late Neolithic assemblages are accidental, not intentional, products), but the presence in the collection from Airhouse and Overhowden of numerous well-executed blade blanks from Levallois-like cores shows that this was clearly not the case (Chapter 2.4). One blade-scraper (BMA 1928) is based on a blank from a Levallois-like core.

The blade-scrapers from the Airhouse/Overhowden assemblage are all relatively short and fairly robust pieces with average dimensions of 43 x 19 x 6 mm (2.3.4-1). They all have distal working-edges, and five of the seven specimens have bilateral blunting. The proximal end of BMA 1931 has been rounded by polish, which relates this piece to the polished-edge implements. BMA 1913 has a distinctly splayed scraper-edge and sharp shoulders. As the surviving retouch of distal fragment BMA 219 is fairly acute, it is possible that this piece is the terminal of a scale-flaked knife. BMA 254 has very robust, steep lateral retouch, and it is uncertain whether this modification represents blunting or additional lateral working-edges.

Eight double-scrapers (that is, scrapers with two opposed scraper-edges, one at each terminal), are all short and flake-based (average dimensions 27 x 27 x 10 mm) (Fig. 16). Five of the six scrapers have full lateral blunting. It is possible that several of the lateral modifications represent additional scraper-edges, one of which (BMA 281.10) is concave. One of the scraper-edges of BMA 785 is denticulated. One double-scraper has had its bulbar area removed by flat retouch.

Two-thirds of the 20 side-scrapers (Fig. 16) are based on simple flakes, whereas six are on blades, and one (BMA 529) is on a bipolar core. Three pieces are based on Levallois-like blanks (BMA 162, 193, 281.61). They are generally slightly elongated, with average dimensions of 30 x 25 x 7 mm (Fig. 18). Four pieces have had their bulbs-of-percussion removed by flat retouch. Several side-scrapers have additional sporadic blunting of various

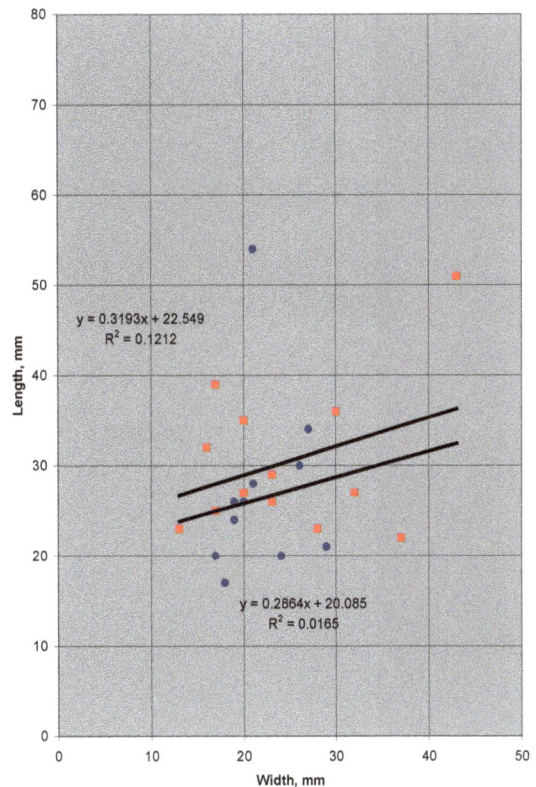

Fig. 18. The dimensions of all intact side-scrapers (red) and side-/end-scrapers (blue).

edges. With 19 pieces, the related side-/end-scrapers are almost as numerous as the side-scrapers. An even larger proportion of this category is flake-based, and only two are based on blades. One (BMA 215) is on an indeterminate core. Two pieces are based on Levallois-like blanks (BMA 105, 350). They are slightly shorter and thicker than the side-scrapers (av. dim.: 26 x 22 x 8 mm; Fig. 18). Only one piece has had its bulbar area deliberately thinned. Five of the side-scrapers and four of the side-/end-scrapers have two lateral working-edges.

One concave scraper (BMA 281.51) has a concave distal scraper-edge; the chord of the working-edge is 20 mm. It is based on a Levallois-like flake, and it has additional bilateral blunting. Three scraper-edge fragments are too small to be referred to a specific scraper type

2.3.5 Polished-edge implements

Although most of the 21 artefacts in this category are in their origin scrapers (Fig. 19), it was chosen to create this separate tool type, as the function of the implements at the end of their use-life was clearly not scraping in the traditional sense.

Seventeen pieces are end-scrapers, which have had their convex distal working-edges transformed by abrasion. Only BMA 686 has had its blunted right lateral side polished, rather than the actual scraper-edge. Apart from

Fig. 19. Polished-edge-implements from Overhowden and Airhouse (BMA 1910, 224, 1927, 165, 281).

Fig. 20. Close-up of the working-edge of one polished-edge implement from Overhowden (BMA 1910).

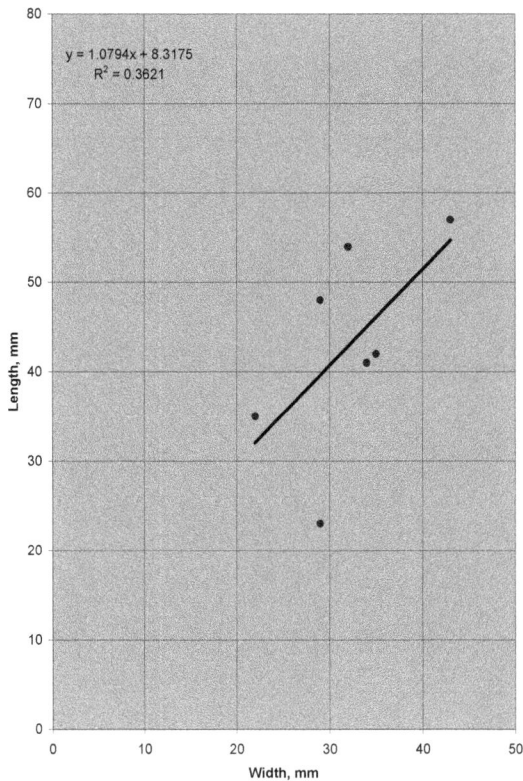

Fig. 21. The dimensions of all intact polished-edge implements.

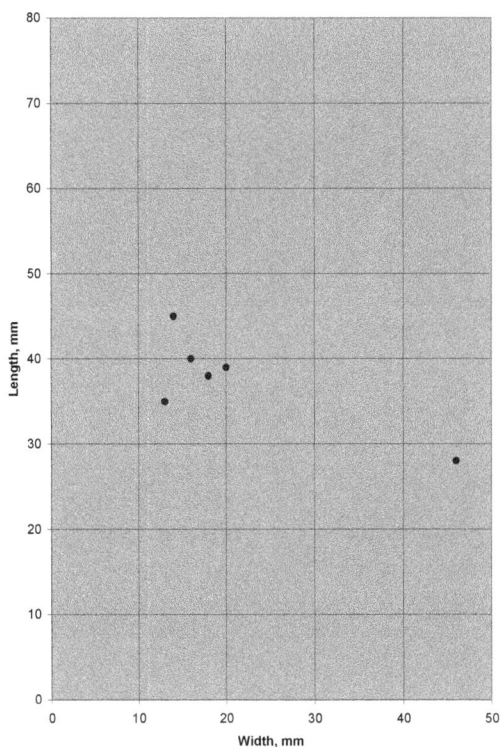

Fig. 22. The dimensions of all intact piercers; as mostly blade piercers have survived intact, a trendline would not be representative of the site's piercers in general, for which reason it was decided not to produce one.

one blade-based piece, these tools are all based on flakes. In some cases, the entire working-edge has been rounded completely by polish, and in other cases only points along the working-edge, or possibly the corners of the working-edge, have been rounded. The polished areas are usually almost mirror-like (Fig. 20), whereas in some cases the polish shows light striations. The polished-edge end-scrapers vary considerably in size, with the largest intact piece measuring 57 x 23 x 12 mm and the smallest 29 x 23 x 7 mm. Six pieces are based on Levallois-like blanks (BMA 166, 252, 686, 842, 1929, 1935).

The category also includes two flake-based side-scrapers with polished working-edges (the intact piece BMA 281.55 measures 32 x 21 x 6 mm), as well as two retouched pieces with polished edges (the intact piece BMA 341 measures 52 x 45 x 12 mm), one being on a flake and one on a blade. One of the latter has polish along one lateral side, whereas the other has polish along one lateral side, as well as at it distal end.

One Levallois-like flake and one ordinary blade with edge-retouch also have rounded and polished edges or corners. The flake (BMA 341) has blunting along its entire circumference, whereas the blade (BMA 119) only has retouch along its left lateral side and along a central break facet. BMA 341 has polish at its distal tip and along the left lateral side, whereas BMA 119 has polish at the corners of the central break. The dimensions of all intact polished-edge implements are shown in Fig. 21.

Three end-scrapers (BMA 165, 686, 1910) with extensive edge-polish were examined for use-wear by Dr Randy Donahue, Bradford University. He determined that they had been used for intensive processing of dry hide, although the exact function of this activity is presently uncertain. The rounded edges cannot have been used for scraping in the traditional sense, as scraping (whether on skin/hides, or harder materials) requires sharp edges.

2.3.6 Piercers

The finds from Airhouse and Overhowden include 11 piercers (Fig. 23), half of which are based on blades, with the other half being flake-based. As indicated by the category's average dimensions (38 x 21 x 6 mm; Fig. 22), mostly blade-based piercers survive intact. The fact that the average length:width ratio of this group is slightly less (1.8:1.0) than that required of blade implements (2:1) is due to the intact survival of one very broad flake piercer (BMA 864; furthest to the right in Fig. 22). One of the blade piercers is on a Levallois-like blank (BMA 114).

The blade piercers commonly have full blunting of both lateral sides, where flake piercers tend to be slightly more idiosyncratic and expedient. In most cases, the piercer tip is distal, but some of the flake-based pieces have their working-ends at suitable corners (eg, BMA 6) or formed on suitable lateral edges (eg, BMA 687). BMA 687 may have had two piercer tips, one of which has broken off. The tip of BMA 888 is clearly abraded from use.

Fig. 23. Piercers from Overhowden and Airhouse (BMA 100, 256, 888).

Fig. 24. Strike-a-lights from Overhowden and Airhouse (BMA 1918, 856, 677, 357).

The two blunted lateral edges of blade piercer BMA 1923 were both retouched simultaneously from the ventral and dorsal faces, but as the modification is not flat (invasive), it would be incorrect to refer to this retouch as bifacial. It could possibly be termed 'pseudo-bifacial'.

2.3.7 Strike-a-lights

Eight strike-a-lights were recovered from the two sites (Fig. 24). Traditionally, these pieces have been referred to in functional terms as either strike-a-lights or fabricators, but it has been chosen to use the former label, as their use-wear corresponds to that found on pieces used for making fire by striking flint against pieces of pyrite (Stapert & Johansen 1999).

Two different fire-making techniques are known, with prehistoric fire-making involving a flint and a piece of pyrite, whereas historic fire-making involved a flint and a mostly bullhorn-shaped steel implement. It is suggested to limit the use of the term 'strike-a-light' to the implements doing the actual striking (subject), and not the material which is being struck (object). This means that, in prehistoric fire-making, the flint is the strike-a-light (as it *strikes* the pyrite), whereas, in historic fire-making, it is not (as it is being *struck* by the steel strike-a-light). The author suggests referring to the struck historic lithics as 'fire-flints'. The fact that the prehistoric and historic fire-making flints are subjects and objects, respectively, results in noticeably different wear-patterns, with the former developing smooth abraded points, whereas the latter developed chipped and crushed edges (Ballin 2007a).

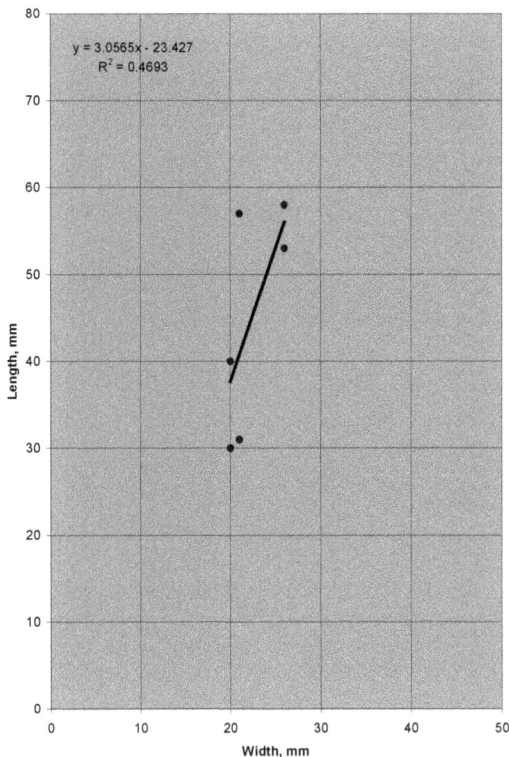

Fig. 25. The dimensions of all intact strike-a-lights.

In her lithic terminology for the Wissey Embayment report, Healy (1996, 76), describes a strike-a-light (fabricator) as: '*Uni- or bifacially flaked, blunted-ended, parallel-sided implement of thick plano-convex or biconvex section, sometimes relatively thin and edge-retouched only, sometimes heavily worn*'. Although she also includes some of the 'rods' from Grimes Graves (Saville 1981, 10, 62) in her definition of strike-a-lights/fabricators, these implements probably represent a different functional category as, among other things, they are characterized by not having terminal abrasion. The specific function of the mainly Middle Bronze Age 'rods' is presently uncertain.

The average dimensions of the six intact pieces from Airhouse and Overhowden (45 x 22 x 14 mm), clearly characterize these implements as elongated and robust (Fig. 25). Most are based on blades (four pieces), with two being flake-based and two are on indeterminate blanks. One blank (BMA 413) was struck from a Levallois-like core.

Two pieces are recycled implements, with BMA 1918 being an exhausted double-edged scale-flaked knife and BMA 1917 an abandoned end-scraper. All pieces in this tool category have one or more worn, usually rounded, terminals, and frequently the steeply blunted edges of these pieces show similar wear patterns.

2.3.8 Serrated pieces and saws

Only five serrated pieces and saws are known from the two sites at Overhowden henge (Fig. 26). It has been chosen to

characterize these related pieces as a particular category, as they occasionally form a very distinct element in Late Neolithic Scottish and British assemblages. Generally, implements with teeth take a number of different forms, such as denticulates (a characteristic element in Middle or Late Bronze Age assemblages; Ballin 2002a, Table 3), serrated pieces and saws. Healy (1996, 76) suggests the following distinctions:

'*Denticulate: piece in the edge of which coarse teeth have been formed, sometimes by the working of contiguous notches, sometimes by the detachment of single flakes*'. This category probably includes a number of expedient tool forms and simple Middle Bronze Age core types, such as, some 'flaked flakes' (Ashton *et al.* 1991).

'*Serrated piece: Straight-sided blank, generally a blade, with one or occasionally both lateral edges finely serrated by the removal of a single chip on either side of each tooth. This effect may be obtained by striking downwards onto the edge of the flake to be serrated with the edge of another flake held at right angles to it*'.

Saw: Coarsely serrated piece, its teeth [...] formed by the removal of two or more small flakes on either side.

The two serrated pieces are both based on blade blanks, whereas the three saws are based on one blade and two elongated flakes. Two pieces survive intact, namely one flake-based and one blade-based saw. The former (BMA 894) measures 38 x 22 x 6 mm, whereas the latter (BMA 115) measures 52 x 23 x 12 mm. Usually, serrated pieces tend to have notably finer serration than saws, but in the present case, the difference is less obvious – the serrated pieces have 5-10 teeth per cm, with the saws having 2-3 teeth per cm. The finest Late Neolithic serrated pieces (such as some pieces from Stoneyhill in Aberdeenshire; Suddaby & Ballin forthcoming) occasionally have 15-20 teeth per cm.

The serrated pieces and the saws are generally characterized by having one serrated lateral side and one opposed blunted side. The teeth of the two serrated pieces and one saw are heavily worn and rounded, and one of the saws (BMA 115) has obvious gloss along both lateral edges. This piece is on a blade from a Levallois-like core. The function of serrated pieces has been discussed by Juel Jensen (1994, 68), who found them difficult to interpret, but who concluded that they probably represent a Neolithic 'non-subsistence related element', such as the refining of fibres, and that they were not used for cutting cereals.

2.3.9 Combined tools

Although most analysts probably perceive this category as simply a practical means of dealing with implements which combine working-edges from different functional categories, it is such a characteristic element of some Late Neolithic assemblages that it should, in this case, be perceived as a formal tool type in its own right.

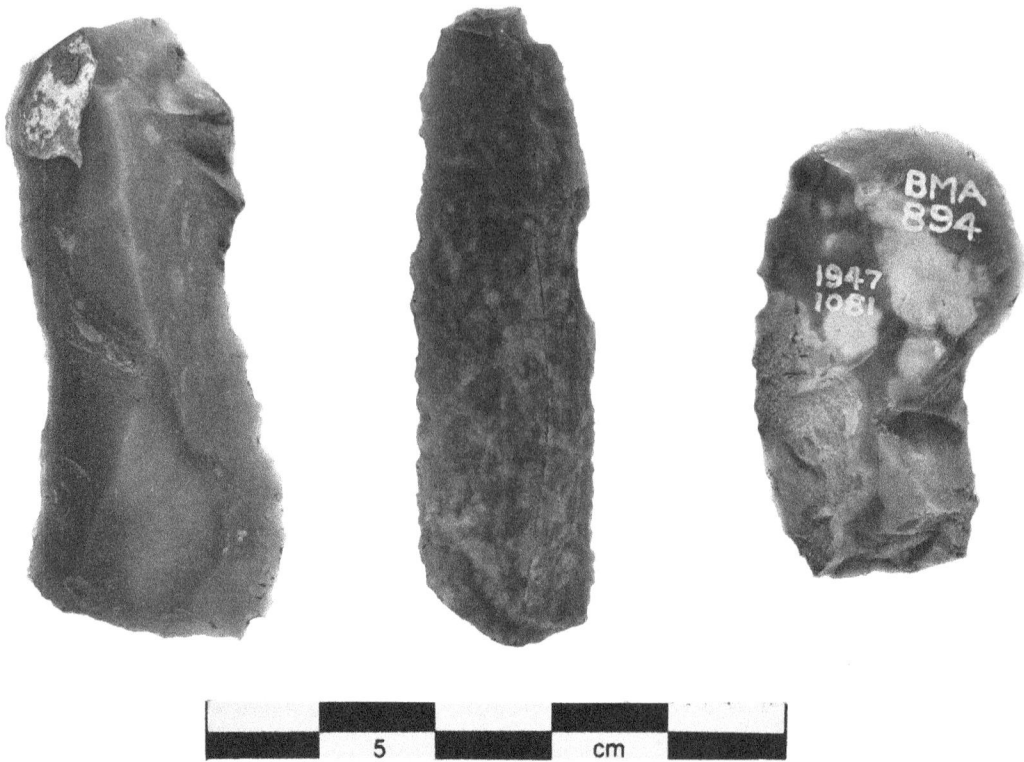

Fig. 26. One serrated piece (BMA 116) and two saws from Airhouse (BMA 115, 894).

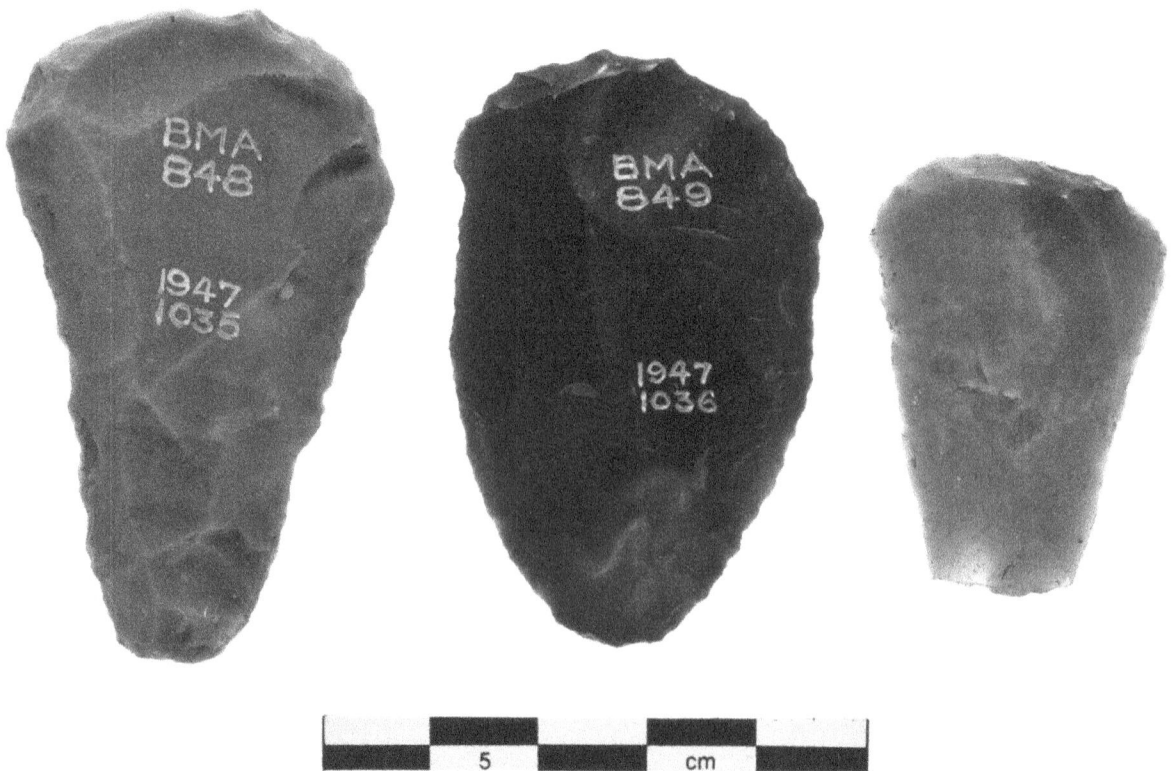

Fig. 27. Combined tools (scale-flaked knives/end-scrapers) from Airhouse (BMA 848, 849, 653).

The finds from Airhouse/Overhowden include 17 combined tools (Fig. 27), and they all combine a knife-edge with the working-edge of another tool form. Fifteen of the knives are scale-flaked knives, whereas two are plano-convex knives. Two of the knives have visible lateral gloss (BMA 103, 281.67). Secondary working-edges include: nine scrapers, six piercers, one strike-a-light, and one polished edge. The scraper-edges include: three blade-scrapers, three short end-scrapers, two polished-edge scrapers, and one double-scraper. Approximately half of the implements are blade-based and the other half flake-based (average dimensions: 44 x 23 x 8 mm; Fig. 28). Five of the combined tools are on Levallois-like blanks (BMA 251, 653, 789, 848, 849).

It is uncertain whether these pieces were originally formed as dual-purpose implements, or whether they represent staged tool biographies, where traditional single-purpose tools were later transformed into more sophisticated implements as a response to *ad hoc* requirements.

2.3.10 Other tool forms

So-called 'other tool forms' (totalling 55 prehistoric pieces and one historical object) include the following implements: two truncated pieces, two notched pieces, one burin, two indeterminate bifacial implements, one indeterminate implement, six fragments with invasive retouch, 41 pieces with simple edge-retouch, and one gunflint. As the gunflint (BMA 281.17) is a historical object (and thus irrelevant to the present analysis), it will not be dealt with below.

The two truncated pieces are one blade with an oblique distal truncation (BMA 117) and one blade with a curved distal truncation (BMA 7). The former is intact and measures 55 x 18 x 6 mm, whereas the latter is a medial-distal fragment which measures 47 x 19 x 6 mm. BMA 117 is based on a blank from a Levallois-like core. Both have various degrees of lateral blunting, and lateral wear of BMA 117 suggests that this piece was used as a knife.

Two notched pieces (BMA 8, 343) are based on relatively plain flakes (av. dim.: 29 x 34 x 7 mm), and they seem to be expedient pieces. BMA 8 is based on a Levallois-like flake. The chord of the notch varies between 9 mm and 11 mm. In addition to the notch, BMA 343 is characterized by having a steep lateral concavity, possibly a scraper-edge.

BMA 790 is the only burin from Airhouse/Overhowden. It is the medial fragment of a flake (31 x 20 x 14 mm), and a broad burin-spall was detached along the left lateral side, from the proximal break. Along the same edge, a series of narrow burin spalls were detached. Use-wear indicates that the edges of the main spall were used as a spoke-shave. This piece is thought to be a residual piece from a visit to the site in the Upper Palaeolithic/Mesolithic period.

Two objects have been classified as fragments of indeterminate bifacial pieces (BMA 1914, 1921). BMA 1914 (53 x 16 x 7 mm) may be a very narrow, elongated

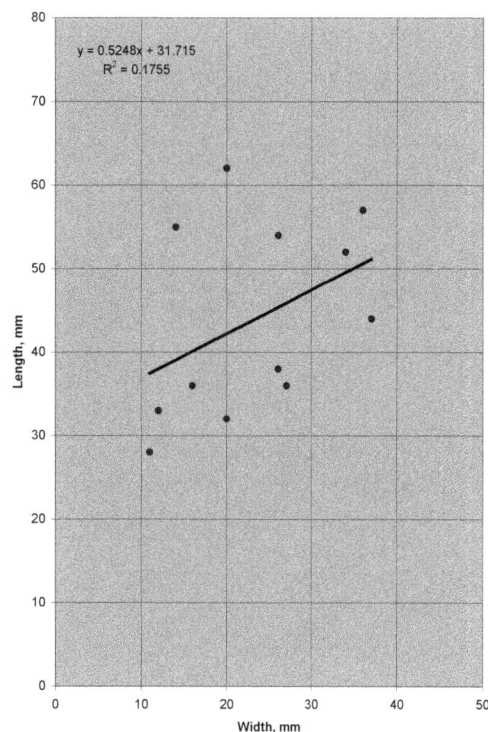

Fig. 28. The dimensions of all intact combined tools.

leaf-shaped point, but the L:W ratio speaks against this interpretation. It is most likely a sophisticated knife form. BMA 1921 (34 x 28 x 9 mm) is either the tip of an Early Bronze Age knife or a strike-a-light. It is uncertain which type of blank was used for the manufacture of these pieces.

BMA 792 has been classified as an indeterminate implement. It is based on a flake (24 x 19 x 13 mm), from which small flakes were removed along the edges, as well as from its ventral face. The function of the piece is unknown. Six pieces (BMA 281.42, 281.48, 281.49, 663, 702, 862) with invasive retouch could not be identified more precisely. They are all based on flakes, and the blank of BMA 281.48 is definitely struck from a Levallois-like core. They form a very heterogeneous group (greatest dimension 20-48 mm), and their modification varies in character, location, and extent. It is suggested that BMA 281.49 may be a rough-out for a chisel-shaped arrowhead; BMA 663 may be a fragment of an indeterminate Neolithic arrowhead; and BMA 862 may be a small knife. A number of relatively large flakes were struck from BMA 702, and it is thought that attempts may have been made to transform this flake into an *ad hoc* Levallois-like core.

Approximately half of 41 pieces with simple edge-retouch are based on blades, with the other half being flake-based. Three pieces are on flakes struck from Levallois-like cores (BMA 660, 854, 886). The 41 retouched implements differ considerably in shape and size (greatest dimension of intact pieces: 24-75 mm), and it is thought that this tool group includes artefacts and fragments of artefacts with different functions. Due to formal similarities with Late

33

Neolithic PTDs, five pieces (BMA 281.11, 531, 716, 867, 1942) may be atypical or expedient variants of such points, or PTD rough-outs.

2.4 Technological approaches

The main purpose of this chapter is to characterize and discuss the Late Neolithic artefacts from Airhouse and Overhowden in technological terms. However, due to the find circumstances – that is, the fact that the material represents selective surface collection and possibly also later selective processes – this presentation and discussion has to be structured slightly differently to the way traditional lithic reports are structured. The key obstacle in this respect is the fact that the Airhouse/Overhowden collection includes practically no debitage (21 pieces) and only three cores.

The two main consequences of this state of affairs are 1) that the technological characterization has to be based almost entirely on the tools and the tool blanks, and 2) that the explanation and discussion of the Late Neolithic Levallois-like technique has to be based largely on finds from other assemblages (eg, Ballin forthcoming a; Suddaby & Ballin forthcoming), where Late Neolithic debitage and, not least, Levallois-like cores were recovered in larger numbers.

The British Late Neolithic technological approaches are, in general, fairly poorly understood, and many erroneous views are in circulation. For this reason, Chapter 2.4 focuses on a number of key issues, such as 1) providing a more precise characterization of the strictly diagnostic Levallois-like technique (Chapter 2.4.1); 2) extricating technological elements and attributes from the tool blanks recovered at Airhouse/Overhowden and characterizing the main operational schema of this assemblage (Chapter 2.4.2); 3) on the basis of the finds from Airhouse/ Overhowden, defining the Late Neolithic industry as a flake or blade industry (or possibly a combined flake/blade industry) (Chapter 2.4.3); and 4) on the basis of the finds from Airhouse/Overhowden, precisely characterizing the Late Neolithic secondary (ie, tool) production (Chapter 2.4.4).

2.4.1 The Levallois-like technique – definition of the main Late Neolithic operational schema

As mentioned above, the almost complete absence of unmodified waste, as well as cores, means that this chapter has to be based almost entirely on finds from other more suitable collections. Amongst these collections, the one from Trench 1 / Grid J at Stoneyhill in Aberdeenshire is the most informative (Ballin forthcoming a; Suddaby & Ballin forthcoming).

Introduction

Through the second half of the 20th century, increasing numbers of 'tortoise' or 'Levallois-like' cores were reported from British Late Neolithic sites. Initially, these cores were perceived as residual Middle Palaeolithic artefacts, but with the mounting evidence for a Late Neolithic link (eg, Moore 1963), this direction of research was soon abandoned. With Manby's (1974) synthetic work on the Late Neolithic of Yorkshire, the case for a Late Neolithic link strengthened further, as Levallois-like cores were found to form part of most larger Late Neolithic assemblages. He also identified a specific type of flake with a faceted platform remnant as the characteristic product of Late Neolithic blank production on Levallois-like cores (Manby 1974, 83).

Since the publication of Manby's work, these cores and their products have been reported from Late Neolithic sites throughout Britain, and they were discussed by Saville (1981, 44-48) in connection with his examination of the Late Neolithic and later Bronze Age assemblages from the flint mines at Grimes Graves in Norfolk. Over the last few decades, Levallois-like cores have been recovered from Late Neolithic settlement sites in East Anglia (eg, Healy 1993; 1996), with further supplements from Yorkshire (eg, Durden 1995). They have also been encountered on Late Neolithic sites throughout Scotland, where they were retrieved from procurement sites, settlement sites, and ritual sites (Chapter 3).

However, no attempts were made at defining the Late Neolithic industry in detail, leaving a number of important questions unanswered. These questions are dealt with immediately below.

The general character and chronology of the post-Palaeolithic Levallois-like approach

In Britain, the Levallois-like approach is associated with two main diagnostic elements, namely PTDs and Impressed Ware / Grooved Ware pottery, indicating a generally Late Neolithic date. Levallois-like cores do not seem to be a feature of the Bronze Age levels at Grimes Graves (Saville 1981, 47), and they are absent from Bronze Age contexts in East Anglia (Healy 1993). They are usually not reported from British Early Neolithic sites (ie, pre-Impressed Ware sites).

The precise dating of British Levallois-like cores is complicated by poorly defined, misleading or erroneous core classification. This problem predominantly relates to assemblages excavated and published prior to 1990, but some 'unhelpful' classification systems are still in circulation. The main problem, in this respect, is the use of the poorly defined core types D and E ('keeled cores') in Clark's core typology (Clark 1960, 216). As discussed in Ballin (forthcoming d), the keeled core categories may include types such as Levallois-like, discoidal and bipolar cores, as well as rough-outs for platform cores with undetached crested guide ridges. In some cases, analysts have expanded Clark's type list to include an additional core type called tortoise, Levallois-like or Levalloisoid (eg, Durden 1995, 425), but in most cases it is necessary

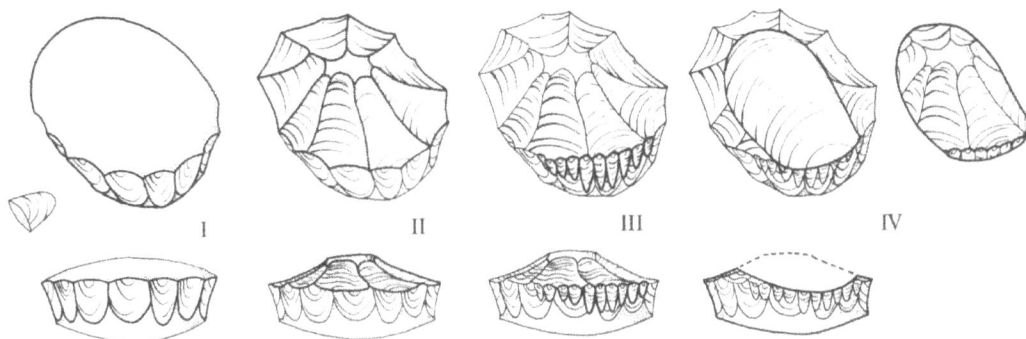

Fig. 29. The operational schema of the Late Acheulean / Mousterian Levalloisian (Roe 1981, Fig. 3:9): I. Basic shaping of nodule; II preparation of domed dorsal surface; III. preparation of faceted striking platform on core; IV. the flake and the struck core, with their characteristic features. Drawn by the late M.H.R. Cook.

to inspect the artefact illustrations of older sites to assess whether any Levallois-like cores were recovered from these locations. It is an additional complication that many older excavation reports do not include illustrations of the cores (or very few: eg, Wainwright & Longworth 1971), or the cores were not dealt with at all (eg, Fell 1952).

In Ballin (forthcoming a), it is argued that the Levallois-like technique may largely be contemporary with the use of Impressed Ware, a period where chisel-shaped arrowheads ruled supreme. However, since the production of this paper, much relevant material has come to light, either in connection with the analysis of old assemblages, or as a result of new excavations. In Scotland, the Levallois-like approach has been proven to form part of Impressed Ware assemblages, such as those of Stoneyhill Trench 1 / Grid J in Aberdeenshire (Suddaby & Ballin forthcoming) and East Lochside in Angus (Johnson & Ballin 2006), but it has also been associated with Grooved Ware assemblages, like those of Barnhouse on Orkney (Ballin forthcoming b), and Midmill in Aberdeenshire (Ballin forthcoming h).

The pitchstone assemblage from Barnhouse was examined in connection with the author's Pitchstone Project (Ballin 2009). This collection includes one Levallois-like core in pitchstone as well as several flakes with finely faceted butts; and the finds from Midmill were recovered from three site areas (an Impressed Ware area, a Grooved Ware area and a Beaker are), where the Impressed Ware area included Levallois-like cores and finely faceted blanks and the Grooved Ware area finely faceted blanks struck off Levallois-like cores.

It is complicated to assess the small number of cases associating Levallois-like cores with oblique arrowheads, either as a result of incomplete reporting, absence of relevant artefact illustrations, or site/assemblage sizes. Some of the sites and assemblages combining Levallois-like cores and oblique arrowheads are fairly large and complex and may reflect multiple visits to the location (eg, Durden 1995; Saville 1981). Although Levallois-like cores were not reported from sites like Durrington Walls (Wainwright & Longworth 1971) and Storey's Bar Road

(Pryor 1978) – both of which are characterized by the presence of large numbers of mainly oblique arrowheads – this may largely be a result of biased recording/classification. The publication of recently excavated finds from Durrington Wall may prove highly significant in this respect (Chan forthcoming).

The Levallois-like operational schema and differences between this schema and the Middle Palaeolithic Levalloisian

It is possible to define the Levallois-like technique in terms of a sequence of technological steps, each of which forms the logical foundation of the following step. Although Roe's Levalloisian schema differs from the Levallois-like schema on a number of points, his step-wise explanation of this approach is helpful in explaining the basic elements of both approaches (Fig. 29).

The Levallois-like approach includes the following elements: First, a relatively crude tortoise-shaped rough-out is formed from a suitable nodule (I-II). Then, a finely faceted platform is shaped at one end (III), along with two lateral guide ridges (this is not a common feature of the Middle Palaeolithic Levalloisian). Blades are then struck from the areas around the two lateral crests (the Levallois-like approach) (Fig. 30), and flakes from the main flaking front (IV). And finally, the Levallois-like core is exhausted completely, occasionally by adding one or more auxiliary platforms, and/or by adding an extra flaking-front (the belly of the original tortoise-shaped rough-out).

The main difference between the Levalloisian and the Levallois-like approaches is probably their general purpose. It is a truism that the primary purpose behind the traditional Levallois technique was to predefine the shape of either oval or pointed flakes removed from the central part of the Levallois cores' flaking-fronts (Fig. 29.IV; Roe 1981, 78-89; also see Inizan *et al.* 1991, Fig.11-13). This relatively limited scope is directly related to the limited tool spectrum, and thereby formal needs, of the later Acheulean and Mousterian periods.

The British Late Neolithic, on the other hand, is characterized by a much more varied tool spectrum, with PTDs, scrapers and cutting implements being the three most important types (eg, Honington [Fell 1952]; Beacon Hill [Moore 1963]; Hunstanton [Healy 1993]; Middle Harling [Healy 1995]; as well as several Scottish assemblages, Chapter 3). As, for example, chisel-shaped arrowheads are based on broad, relatively thin flakes, and cutting implements (knives and serrated pieces) on long slender blades, it is most likely that the Late Neolithic Levallois-like approach had a dual purpose (*contra* Durden 1995, 411), namely the production of two distinctly different types of blanks on the same core type: blades from the crested areas of the cores; and broad flakes from the centre of the flaking-fronts (Fig. 30).

This suggestion is supported by the fact that, at Stoneyhill Trench 1 / Grid J (Suddaby & Ballin forthcoming), many crested blades were produced (11 pieces, or almost 2% of the debitage), and one of the two serrated pieces has a surviving dorsal crest. The fact that the serrated pieces of British Late Neolithic industries are mainly on elegant blades was also noted by Healy (1993, 33; 1996, 37). The scrapers of this material culture are generally on oval, thick flakes, and although the robust nature of many of these scrapers suggests that they were based on waste flakes from the decortication of the cores, the generally high proportion of tertiary pieces (*c.* 70%) indicates that most were probably based on deliberately produced flake tool blanks (see below).

The common perception (eg, Green 1984, 84) of Levallois-like cores being specialized cores for the production of PTD blanks is rejected by Healy (1985, 194) in her report on the Tye Field flints. She writes: '*Green's suggestion (1984, 84) that flakes from prepared [Levallois-like cores] were struck as blanks for chisel arrowheads would hold good for Honington, but not for the other East Anglian industries in which chisel arrowheads are scarce or lacking. Nor would it hold good for those areas and industries in which chisel arrowheads are abundant and [Levallois-like cores] scarce. For reasons which are now unclear, what was elsewhere an occasional or specialized knapping practice seems to have become more general within the region*'.

The different purposes of the two core types, Levallois cores and Levallois-like cores, have a direct effect on the associated operational schemas, as the first step of the Levallois approach is to detach one or more flakes from the central part of the core's main flaking-front, whereas the first step of the Levallois-like approach (Fig. 30) is to detach the two lateral crests and, usually, a series of blades immediately next to and under the crests. One of the 'design flaws' of the Levallois and Levallois-like approaches is that the flaking-front's flatness tends to produce many more plunging flakes than in connection with other reduction techniques. This flaw is counteracted (but not removed) by detaching the crests first, as this makes the flaking-front more domed and slightly less prone to plunging. In the future, this hypothesis should be tested by the refitting of a suitable Late Neolithic assemblage.

In terms of the general shape of the two core types, there are no fundamental differences, but the tortoise rough-outs of the later approach tend to have been more extensively prepared, with more carefully, more finely faceted platforms, and more regular crests. The main differences appear in the later stages of the two operational schemas, largely as a consequence of the Levallois-like approach's partial focus on the production of crested blades and ordinary blades. The detachment of crests and their immediate surroundings removes major parts of the cores' lateral sides, and where a Levallois core frequently has surviving scars from the initial preparation of the core laterals (Fig. 30), in most cases, these scars have been removed from the lateral sides of the Levallois-like cores. To the inexperienced specialist it may be difficult to acknowledge the later stages of Levallois-like cores for what they truly are, but these 'flat cores' are quite characteristic pieces (see for example the characterization of the lithic finds from Stoneyhill; Suddaby & Ballin forthcoming).

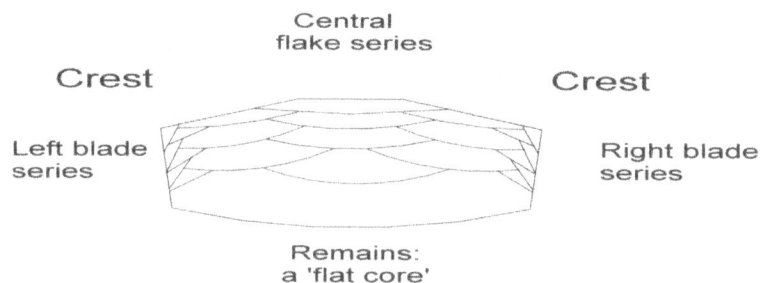

Fig. 30. The Levallois-like reduction sequence: first, a number of crested blades and ordinary blades are detached from the core's flanks, near the two lateral guide ridges; then, a series of flakes are detached from the relatively flat central flaking front.

The most secure way of recognising the application of Levallois-like reduction is by carrying out full assemblage analyses, and by the combined recovery of tortoise core rough-outs, exhausted 'flat cores', crested blades, finely faceted flakes and blades (see following section), PTDs and typical Late Neolithic cutting implements. Usually, the lustre of the pieces will define them as either Palaeolithic or post-Palaeolithic specimens, as most of the former have a characteristic sheen, whereas most of the latter have reasonably fresh surfaces.

A more precise definition of the platform remnants of Late Neolithic Levallois-like blanks

As clearly stated by Manby (1974, 83), '... *narrow flake facets across the butt of flakes and tools ...*' are a characteristic feature of Late Neolithic assemblages. This trait is not always a dominating feature, as proven by Saville's (1981, 41) demonstration of low 'faceted butt ratios' in several sub-assemblages at Grimes Graves (*c.* 4-10%), but the main point is that these finely faceted pieces are *present* in Late Neolithic assemblages, whereas they are usually *absent* in assemblages from other prehistoric periods (apart from certain Upper Palaeolithic assemblages; cf. Ballin *et al.* forthcoming). The notable difference between the low ratios (*c.* 4-10%) of the Grimes Graves Late Neolithic levels and the high ratios (*c.* 50–60%) of, for example, the Late Neolithic Stoneyhill assemblages (Trench 1 / Grid J and Cairn 7/17 (Pit 7183); Suddaby & Ballin forthcoming) may reflect the different characters of the sites, with Grimes Graves being mainly a quarry-cum-factory site, whereas the Stoneyhill assemblages represent domestic and ritual depositions. Late Neolithic Scottish assemblages are generally characterized by fairly high ratios of finely faceted tool blanks (Chapters 2.3-4 and 3).

The main problem relating to the diagnosticity of the characteristic Late Neolithic flake and blade butts is the fact that in some reports lithic analysts have excluded the word 'finely' from the description of these faceted platform remnants, and it may be claimed that a given assemblage includes Late Neolithic elements due to the presence of *faceted* butts. This is an unfortunate simplification, as faceted platform remnants are produced in practically all traditional lithic industries, where rejuvenation of platforms by detaching core tablets is practiced. Not all core tablets are complete, either by accident or by choice, and whenever partial core tablets are removed from platform surfaces, subsequent blanks tend to have faceted platform remnants. Obviously, the larger the platform remnant, the larger the possibility of that area becoming faceted. In other industries, small hinged flakes may have been detached immediately behind the platform-edge, either to adjust the platform-edge or to provide a more suitable 'seat' for a pressure-flaking punch, and the subsequent blanks from these cores may also acquire faceted platform remnants.

As suggested above, the fine faceting of Late Neolithic core platforms and flake/blade butts should probably be seen as a form of horizontal trimming, and it is practically

indistinguishable from traditional vertical trimming. Only *finely* faceted platform remnants are diagnostic of the British Late Neolithic.

The basic elements ('modules') of Late Neolithic flint-knapping

Even accepting that many of the keeled cores of the published Late Neolithic assemblages may be Levallois-like, it is obvious that flakes were also produced on other core forms. At Beacon Hill (Moore 1963, 194), for example, the flint collection includes 65 Levallois-like cores, as well as 100 more traditional fluted cores. Some of the traditional core types recovered from Late Neolithic sites may be exhausted Levallois-like cores, where the detachment of the lateral crests and the lateral sides have made positive identification difficult, and some may be adaptations of damaged Levallois-like cores (both examples are represented in the assemblage from Stoneyhill Trench 1 / Grid J; Suddaby & Ballin forthcoming). However, there is little doubt that some production of ordinary flakes took place on traditional platform cores.

At present, it is not possible to assess the operational schemas of most published assemblages, as the majority of these were classified according to Clark's type schema from 1960, but the assemblage from, for example, Stoneyhill Trench 1 / Grid J (ibid.) suggests that parallel production on traditional core types was less common than blank production on Levallois-like cores. In several cases, seemingly traditional cores are based on alteration or exhaustion of Levallois-like cores, and maybe as little as a handful of platform cores (roughly 10%) are traditional cores formed specifically for the production of simple flakes. The frequent fine faceting of platforms on both core types indicates contemporaneity between traditional cores and their Levallois-like counterparts, and it supports the suggestion that many apparently ordinary Late Neolithic platform cores may represent the exhausted remains of Levallois-like cores. The varying ratios between Levallois-like and traditional cores on Late Neolithic sites may be a reflection of different site activities, or Levallois-like cores may be particularly common in certain Late Neolithic phases. This should be explored in connection with the analysis of future Late Neolithic assemblages.

2.4.2 Levallois-like elements identified in the Airhouse/ Overhowden assemblage

Although only 21 unmodified flakes and blades were recovered from Airhouse and Overhowden, it should be noted that two of those are Levallois-like blades (BMA 679, 772). The collection also includes three cores (BMA 643, 644, 685), all of which are Levallois-like pieces.

Table 11 quantifies the various tool categories in terms of their ratios of Levallois-like attributes (finely faceted platform remnants). Four categories (scale-flaked knives, polished-edge implements, serrated pieces/saws and combined tools) have very high ratios (*c.* 20-30%),

	Quantity	Per cent of group total
LN arrowheads	5	2
Scale-flaked knives	7	20
Short end-scrapers	16	14
Blade-scrapers	1	14
Side- and side-/end-scrapers	5	13
Concave scrapers	1	100
Polished-edge implements	7	32
Piercers	1	9
Strike-a-lights	1	13
Serrated pieces/saws	1	20
Combined tools	5	29
Other tool forms	6	11
TOTAL	**56**	**9**

Table 11. Ratio of identifiable Levallois-like tool blanks per tool category.

whereas most of the other categories have somewhat lower ratios (*c.* 10-15%). Some categories, like LN arrowheads (2%) and plano-convex knives (0%), have exceedingly low ratios, but this is probably due to these pieces having been extensively modified, frequently by totally covering invasive retouch or at least by extensive modification of all or most edges, such as, in the case of PTDs, L3 and L4 (Fig. 2). Other categories, like concave scrapers (100%), have exceedingly high ratios, but in these cases very low population sizes (only one concave scraper was found) may have skewed the outcome.

The most important single factor influencing these ratios is the fragmentation of the artefacts from Airhouse and Overhowden. Obviously, it is only possible to determine whether a piece has a finely faceted butt if the platform remnant survives, and in many cases it does not. Whether this essential part survives or not is due to a number of factors, such as the fineness of the individual piece, and the force applied in connection with the use of this piece. In some cases, only *c.* 40-55% of a specific category has a surviving proximal end (eg, blade-scrapers, polished-edge implements, piercers, and serrated pieces/saws), whereas other categories are characterized by ratios in the order of *c.* 65-75% (scale-flaked knives, short end-scrapers, side- and side-/end-scrapers, strike-a-lights, and combined tools). If artefact fragmentation is taken into consideration, it may be assumed that the ratios mentioned above (fine faceting) would have been approximately 25-50% higher before fragmentation.

If this factor is taken into account, as well as the possibility that a small proportion of cortical tool blanks may be waste flakes from the decortication of Levallois-like cores (for which reason they would not have finely faceted butts), it appears increasingly likely that most of the implements from Airhouse and Overhowden were produced on blanks from earlier (without fine faceting) or later stages (with fine faceting) of the Levallois-like operational schema.

The same conclusion was reached in connection with the analysis of the finds from Trench 1 / Grid J at Stoneyhill (Suddaby & Ballin forthcoming), where a large number of unmodified waste and cores survived. It is quite likely that some less sophisticated, traditional operational schemas were also followed at Airhouse and Overhowden (as was the case at Stoneyhill), but due to the composition of the finds (no unmodified flakes and blades, and almost no cores) this remains an unverified assumption. The fact that some tool blanks have plain, or crudely faceted, platform remnants does not necessarily define those as non-Levallois-like, as some platforms on Levallois-like cores, may have been prepared in an expedient manner by 'sloppy' prehistoric knappers.

2.4.3 Flakes vs blades

As the assemblages from Airhouse and Overhowden (Table 1) include almost no debitage, the only way of assessing the primary technology responsible for these assemblages is by analysing their tool blanks.

The composition of the Airhouse/Overhowden collection's arrowheads suggests that a minimum of 80% of the assemblages may be Late Neolithic, and the composition of the tool blanks in Table 12 therefore probably provides a realistic picture of the Late Neolithic technology of the Airhouse and Overhowden sites. Combined, the two assemblages have a blade ratio (or lamellar index) of 25%. According to Bordes & Gaussen (1970), a blade ratio of 20% is required to classify an industry as a blade industry, suggesting that the Airhouse/Overhowden assemblage is the product of a blade industry. In the author's view, the approach of Bordes & Gaussen is too mechanistic, and the classification of an industry as a flake or blade industry should not be based entirely on a ratio. Instead, it should be based on whether it could be argued that blades are intentional products of that industry or not (that is, a fuller understanding of the operational schema in question),

	Quantity	Per cent
Flakes	263	73
Blades	88	25
Indeterminate pieces	1	-
Cores	8	2
TOTAL	**360**	**100**

Table 12. Airhouse and Overhowden: Definable tool blanks.

	Flake:blade ratio
LN arrowheads	100:00
Knives	37:63
Scrapers	92:08
Polished-edge implements	90:10
Strike-a-lights	83:17
Serrated pieces/saws	40:60

Table 13. Flake:blade ratios of the most important tool categories from Airhouse and Overhowden.

whatever the collection's blade ratio. The regularity of the Airhouse and Overhowden blade blanks (ie, their parallel lateral sides and dorsal arrises) clearly define these as intentional (ie, non-random) blades.

There is no doubt that most of the blades from the two sites are Late Neolithic, as 1) they were almost exclusively (90%) detached by the application of hard percussion (Butler 2005, 157; also, Suddaby & Ballin forthcoming), and 2) many were struck from Levallois-like cores (almost one-quarter of all blade blanks with intact proximal ends). Mesolithic and Early Neolithic blades were generally detached by soft percussion (Butler 2005, 121), and the Levallois-like technique is entirely a Late Neolithic phenomenon (Chapters 2.4.1-2).

The fact that the cores were carefully decorticated before commencement of blade production is suggested by the distribution of the blade blanks across the various stages of the reduction sequence. No primary blades were recovered, and tertiary blades (that is, completely decorticated blades) make up as much as 70%. Secondary, or partially decorticated, blades make up 30% of all blade blanks. Even if it is taken into account that less spectacular tools were deselected either in the field or after collection, these figures indicate that a relatively sophisticated, staged operational schema was adhered to. However, the flake blanks are characterized by almost the same composition, with almost no primary flakes and approximately 70% tertiary pieces, suggesting that they are not simply utilized waste flakes, but that they may be as carefully decorticated (ie, intentional) pieces as the blade blanks. This indicates, that the Late Neolithic industry responsible for the two

assemblages aimed not simply to produce one type of target blanks, the blades (with the flakes representing waste), but that two different types of target (ie, intentional) blanks were produced – regular blades and broad flakes.

Table 13 shows the flake and blade ratios of the Airhouse/ Overhowden collection's most important tool categories. These ratios indicate that different blanks may have been manufactured for different purposes, with arrowheads being entirely on flakes (100%), and cutting implements (knives, serrated pieces and saws) largely on blades (c. 60%). The categories scrapers, polished-edge implements and strike-a-lights are mainly on flakes but include 10-20% blade blanks. In several cases, the flake and blade versions of these tools (for example, flake and blade scrapers) are so morphologically different that they may have been intended for different functions, and, most likely, the choice of blank was non-random. This supports the above suggestion that the industry responsible for the Airhouse and Overhowden assemblages is not a flake *or* a blade industry, but an industry focusing on the production of specialized flakes and blades for a number of separate purposes.

This view clearly breaks with traditional opinions on the technological status of the British Late Neolithic period. In the archaeological literature, the Late Neolithic lithic technology has frequently been characterized as simple, and it has generally been perceived as a flake industry, as there are clearly fewer blades in Late Neolithic assemblages than in earlier collections. Pitts & Jacobi (1979, 176), for example, write that '... *[the] scarcity of blades after the Early Neolithic in some domestic assemblages may then reflect this decline in commonly possessed knapping skills*'. A similar view is expressed by Butler (2005, 155), who writes that '... *the whole process [is] seeing a general decline in care and quality*' and he claims that, for example, blade-scrapers are no longer produced (ibid., 166). The claim that blade production was phased out at the Early-Late Neolithic transition has also been expressed by this author and, as demonstrated above, this was not the case.

It could be suggested that these views are due to different archaeologists defining the Late Neolithic in different ways, and if the quotes above are based on the perception that the Late Neolithic period is synonymous with the period during which Grooved Ware was used, these authors would be dealing with the later phase of the period as it is defined by the present author (Chapter 1.4). However, recently recovered Scottish assemblages, such as Barnhouse on Orkney (Ballin forthcoming b) and Midmill in Aberdeenshire (Ballin forthcoming h), clearly show that blades were produced well into the Grooved Ware period, and it is presently uncertain exactly when the production of this type of blank was phased out – we just know that it happened prior to the Late Neolithic/Early Bronze Age transition (as suggested by the finds from Stoneyhill Cairn 7/17 (Pit 7183); Suddaby & Ballin forthcoming).

2.4.4   Secondary production (tools)

Late Neolithic tool production is surprisingly distinct, and it is characterized by the following identifiable elements:

- Composition of the tool category;
- Preferred tool blanks, and tool blank specialization;
- Modification of the tool blanks' bulbar area (removal, thinning or narrowing);
- Working-edge modification forms (retouch and grinding/polish); and
- Functional combinations/implement recycling.

The composition of the Airhouse/Overhowden tools was touched upon in Chapters 2.1 and 2.3, and summarized in Tables 1 and 2. The most dominant tool categories at the two sites are arrowheads (38%), scrapers (28%) and knives (7%), but as indicated in Chapter 3, arrowheads are usually considerably less common in Late Neolithic assemblages than at Airhouse/Overhowden. Other relatively common tool types are polished-edge implements, piercers, strike-a-lights and combined tools. Diagnostic tool forms include PTDs (strictly Late Neolithic), polished-edge implements (strictly Late Neolithic) and strike-a-lights (more common in Late Neolithic than in earlier or later contexts).

As described above, the collection's tools are based partly on flakes and partly on blades, with both having been manufactured by the application of hard percussion. Some blade blanks are relatively delicate, but due to the applied form of percussion, most are fairly robust, with pronounced bulbs of percussion. A significant proportion, if not most, of the two sites' tool blanks were struck from Levallois-like cores, and apart from those cases where the proximal end has been removed accidentally or deliberately, or where the proximal end has been heavily modified, these blanks usually display finely faceted platform remnants.

It was argued above, that the Late Neolithic operational schema probably includes tool blank specialization (Table 13), with some tool categories being based almost entirely on flakes and others on blades. However, it also appears that a form of specialization took place within some tool categories with, for example, some scrapers having been deliberately manufactured on broad flakes (eg, the typical Late Neolithic horseshoe scrapers) and others on long blades.

Modification of the bulbar area seems to have been a common feature at Airhouse and Overhowden, probably to facilitate hafting. In two cases (BMA 186, 212), the bulb itself is missing, but it is thought that these bulbs were detached accidentally (*erraillure* flakes) as a result of the significant force (hard percussion) applied to detach them from their parent cores. The bulbar end of BMA 162 (a side-/end-scraper) may have been snapped off deliberately. However, in most cases (18 pieces) modification of the bulbar area was carried out either by retouch of the lateral sides or by retouch of one or both faces, proximal end. The most common form of bulbar modification is the removal

of several flat ventral flakes (BMA 35, 112, 119, 245, 363, 396, 401, 892), but in two cases (BMA 256, 257), the bulbar area was thinned by detaching one large ventral flake. The bulbar area of BMA 157 was modified by invasive retouch of both faces, proximal end. Two implements (BMA 270, 307) have had their bulbar area thinned by the removal of ventral flakes by bipolar (hammer-and-anvil) technique, although the use of the bipolar approach is not a characteristic feature of the Airhouse/Overhowden collection. And five pieces (BMA 86, 114, 298, 393, 425) have had their bulbar area diminished in size by bilateral edge-retouch.

All industries from (and including) the Early Neolithic to the Early Bronze Age embrace the use of invasive retouch as a means of modifying tool blanks into tools. This is also the case in the present situation, and several of the most typical Late Neolithic implement types are based on the formation of tool working-edges by invasive retouch, such as PTDs, knives and combined tools. The scrapers, piercers, strike-a-lights and serrated pieces/saws are shaped largely by the application of edge-retouch. Although the working-edge of most scrapers is steep, 25 scrapers (14%) from Airhouse and Overhowden are characterized by acute or relatively acute scraper-edges. This feature separates Late Neolithic and Early Bronze Age industries from pre Late Neolithic industries.

However, the most distinctly Late Neolithic form of tool modification is the polish found along the working-edges of some knives and scrapers. The Airhouse/Overhowden assemblage includes two knives which had their cutting-edges formed by polish, one being a so-called discoidal knife (BMA 795) and the other a polished-edge blade-knife (BMA 1909). The collection also embraces 21 mostly scrapers with partial or complete polish of their working-edges (polished-edge implements). This polish may represent a form of use-wear rather than deliberate modification.

As stated in Chapter 2.3.8, it is uncertain whether the collection's 17 combined tools represent mental templates, where combined tools (mostly knives/scrapers and knives/piercers) were formed as such from the outset – that is, in anticipation of specific future needs – or whether they represent recycling, where one spent tool form was transformed into a new tool form. As the inhabitants at Airhouse and Overhowden seem to have had access to abundant resources of Yorkshire flint, there would have been little reason to adhere to strict recycling policies, and it is probably most likely that the combined tools represent specific 'mini tool kits', that is, different forms of prehistoric 'Swiss army knives'. These pieces were only recovered from the Airhouse site, and not from the Overhowden site, but, as stated by Butler (2005, 168), they definitely represent a characteristic element of Late Neolithic tool production. According to Butler (ibid.), the combinations usually incorporate a scraper-part, but at Airhouse the universal part was clearly the knife-edge, with the most common other parts being scraper-edges and piercer tips. Although combination tools may occasionally be recovered from Early Neolithic, as well as Early Bronze Age, contexts, a *large* proportion of combination tools is a diagnostic feature of Late Neolithic assemblages.

2.5 Dating

The finds from Airhouse and Overhowden may be dated by three key elements, namely 1) raw material preferences, 2) tool typology and 3) technological attributes.

2.5.1 Raw material preferences

Diagnostic elements associated with the collection's lithic raw materials are 1) the relative proportions of flint and non-flint, and 2) the relative proportions of grey flint and dark-brown flint. The fact that the finds from Airhouse and Overhowden are almost entirely in flint (2-5% chert) suggests a generally Late Neolithic date, with most of the chert implements being diagnostic Early Neolithic or Early Bronze Age pieces. Only one PTD is in chert (*c.* 0.5%), whereas 11 leaf-shaped arrowheads (34%) are in this material, and three barbed-and-tanged arrowheads (11%). A small discoidal scraper in chert (BMA 787) may also date to the Early Bronze Age period. In general, Early Neolithic assemblages from South Lanarkshire and the Scottish Borders are almost completely dominated by chert (eg, Glentaggart, South Lanarkshire; Ballin & Johnson 2005), although with increasing flint ratios towards the shores of the North Sea. Statistically representative, unmixed Early Bronze Age assemblages from this region are rare, but the composition of diagnostic stray finds indicates that they may be characterized by a higher chert ratio than Late Neolithic finds, but a lower chert ratio than Early Neolithic ones.

The likely inclusion of some residual Early Neolithic pieces is supported by the retrieval of three pitchstone artefacts (BMA 705, 775, 897) from Airhouse. In his analysis of the Scottish prehistoric exchange in Arran pitchstone, the author (Ballin 2009) demonstrated that, outside Arran, Argyll & Bute and Orkney, pitchstone was predominantly exchanged during the first half of the Early Neolithic period.

As shown in Table 3, the flints from Airhouse and Overhowden represent three main types, namely grey (76%), dark-brown (17%) and 'others' (6%). The latter group is mainly local pebble flint in colours such as cream, yellow, orange and red. This type of flint is a characteristic element of Mesolithic and Early Neolithic collections from the Scottish Borders (cf., Mulholland 1970, 85). The grey and dark-brown flint forms are generally associated with Late Neolithic importation (ibid.), and at Airhouse and Overhowden practically all tool types datable to the Late Neolithic (PTDs, polished-edge implements, combined tools, pieces from Levallois-like cores, etc.) are in this material (cf., Callander 1928, 172; Stevenson 1948, 181).

The different flint compositions of the Airhouse/ Overhowden PTDs indicate that, in Scotland, earlier Late Neolithic assemblages may be characterized by a relatively low ratio of dark-brown flint and later Late Neolithic assemblages by a notably higher ratio. The recovered chisel-shaped arrowheads, for example, have low dark-brown flint ratios (<30%) and some oblique arrowhead types up to *c.* 80% (Fig. 3). Although both assemblages appear to include finds from the earlier and later parts of the Late Neolithic period (Chapter 2.5.2), the Airhouse assemblage is clearly dominated by earlier Late Neolithic material and Overhowden by later Late Neolithic material, with relative proportions of grey and dark-brown flint of 80:14% and 57:35%, respectively.

It is uncertain exactly when the exchange in Yorkshire flint commenced and stopped, but the fact that some obvious Early Neolithic and Early Bronze Age tool types (for example, arrowheads) are in grey flint suggests a gradual start in the later part of the Early Neolithic period and a slow decline in the earlier stages of the Early Bronze Age period.

2.5.2 Tool typology

The finds from Airhouse and Overhowden embrace a considerable number of strictly diagnostic tool types, such as different forms of arrowheads, adzeheads and knives, as well as discoidal knives, polished-edge knives, polished-edge implements, strike-a-lights, and combined tools. A solitary burin (BMA 790) represents pre-Neolithic residuality and a gunflint (BMA 281.17) later intrusion.

The arrowheads from the two sites are PTDs (80%), leaf-shaped points (11%) and barbed-and-tanged points (9%), suggesting that the locations' Late Neolithic artefacts may outnumber Early Neolithic and Early Bronze Age pieces by a factor of four to one (Table 10). As mentioned in Chapter 2.3.1, the leaf-shaped arrowheads include 15% late kite-shaped pieces, and this fact, in conjunction with the fact that the barbed-and-tanged arrowheads include no late Kilmarnock points, indicates that the Airhouse/ Overhowden collection was deposited mainly during the Late Neolithic period, but with some finds dating to the later part of the Early Neolithic period and some to the earlier part of the Early Bronze Age.

In Table 7, the PTDs are broken down into main sub-categories, with chisel-shaped arrowheads making up approximately half of all PTDs, and deviating pieces/ oblique arrowheads approximately 38% (the remainder of the PTDs are either rough-outs or unclassifiable/atypical specimens). This suggests that earlier Late Neolithic pieces may outnumber later pieces, but if it is accepted that some chisel-shaped pieces may date to the later phase of the Late Neolithic (as indicated by the finds from Storey's Bar Road; Pryor 1978), earlier pieces probably outnumber later pieces by slightly less than indicated by the proportions given in Table 7.

However, the two assemblages are composed slightly differently, with the finds from Airhouse being dominated by chisel-shaped arrowheads (57%) and those from Overhowden by oblique arrowheads and arrowheads of the deviating group (70%). This suggests that the former assemblage is likely to be dominated by finds from the earlier part of the Late Neolithic period, whereas the latter assemblage is dominated substantially by finds from the later part of the Late Neolithic period. In Chapter 2.3.1, the following general PTD chronology was suggested: 1) chisel-shaped arrowheads were introduced early in the Impressed Ware period (eg, East Lochside and Stoneyhill Trench 1 / Grid J; Johnson & Ballin 2006; Suddaby & Ballin forthcoming); 2) then, oblique arrowheads were introduced at the beginning of the Grooved Ware period, and the two types and functions probably co-existed for a time (eg, Storey's Bar Road, Pit W17; Pryor 1978, 104-5); and 3) finally, chisel-shaped arrowheads were phased out and oblique arrowheads reigned supreme (eg, Durrington Walls and Tye Field; Wainwright & Longworth 1971; Healy 1985).

The combined Airhouse/Overhowden assemblage only includes one axe-/adzehead (BMA 41), and the treatment of its working-edge and two faces defines it as an edge-polished adzehead. With its straight, diverging lateral sides it differs from the highly diagnostic concave-sided axe- and adzeheads of Seamer/Duggleby Type. The latter are generally dated to the earlier part of the Late Neolithic period and associated with the Towthorpe burial tradition and Impressed Ware (Manby 1974, 93). However, edge-polished axe- and adzeheads are in themselves considered diagnostic of the Late Neolithic period *sensu largo*; the present specimen corresponds quite precisely to a 'marginally edge-ground' axehead from Bessingby in Yorkshire (Manby 1979, 70).

The knife forms are generally more or less diagnostic. Discoidal knives were first discussed by Clark (1932b), who dated them to the Late Neolithic period. They are usually associated with Grooved Ware pottery (Manby 1974, 86; Butler 2005, 172). Most polished-edge knives appear to date to the Impressed Ware period (Manby 1974, 8). Scale-flaked and plano-convex knives occur throughout the Early Neolithic – Early Bronze Age period (Butler 2005, 129, 170), but only the Late Neolithic forms are based predominantly on blade blanks. At Airhouse and Overhowden, two-thirds of the scale-flaked knives are on blades and all plano-convex knives are blade-based. In contrast, most knives from the Early Neolithic and the Early Bronze Age are based on flakes.

Polished-edge implements are mostly end- or side-scrapers with partial or complete polish of their working-edges and, on occasion, other edges, corners and ridges may have been polished. They seem to date exclusively to the Late Neolithic period. At Airhouse/Overhowden, 21 pieces were recovered, and they are well-known from most other substantial Late Neolithic assemblages, such as Windmill Hill (Smith 1965, 105), West Kennet Avenue (ibid., 241)

and several Grooved Ware sites in Yorkshire (Manby 1974, 83), but they do not appear to have been recovered from, for example, Durrington Walls (Wainwright & Longworth 1971, Table XXVIII).

Solitary strike-a-lights (or fabricators) may be recovered from most prehistoric periods, but they are particularly common in the Late Neolithic. Again, the preference for robust blades as tool blanks (at Airhouse/Overhowden: four of six identifiable pieces) identifies these pieces as Late Neolithic.

As stated by Butler (2005, 168), combination tools may be found throughout the Early Neolithic – Early Bronze Age period, but they are particularly common in the Late Neolithic. At Airhouse, 17 implements of this type were recovered. As suggested above, in the Late Neolithic period these artefacts may represent specific pre-defined tool forms, where in other industries they probably represent expedient ways of recycling spent implements by adding a new working-end.

2.5.3 Technological attributes

Two technological elements are of importance to the dating of the finds from Airhouse/Overhowden, namely 1) the fact that most of the assemblage is based on the application of the Levallois-like technique (Chapters 2.4.1-2), and 2) the combined use of flakes and blades as tool blanks (Chapter 2.4.3).

In Chapters 2.4.1 and 2.4.2, it was argued that the bulk of the tools from the two sites are based on blanks from Levallois-like cores, possibly with a small proportion of blanks deriving from traditional platform-cores. As explained in the introduction of Chapter 2.4.1, the Levallois-like technique is exclusively Late Neolithic, with the related Levalloisian technique dating to the Middle Palaeolithic. As no tool forms suggest a Palaeolithic date, this defines the Airhouse/Overhowden assemblage as predominantly Late Neolithic.

The notable presence of broad blades at Airhouse and Overhowden is significant to the dating of the finds:

- The presence of finely faceted platform remnants on many blades establishes once and for all that blades were produced as part of the Levallois-like approach, and that blades form part of the main Late Neolithic operational schema (Ballin forthcoming a);
- The fact that approximately 90% of the Airhouse/Overhowden blades were detached by the application of hard percussion indicates that a very high proportion of the finds from these two sites were produced after the Mesolithic/Early Neolithic period, where soft percussion was the dominant approach (Butler 2005, 121);
- The presence of blades in itself indicates a date prior to the Early Bronze Age period, which was characterized by the production of elongated flakes, with

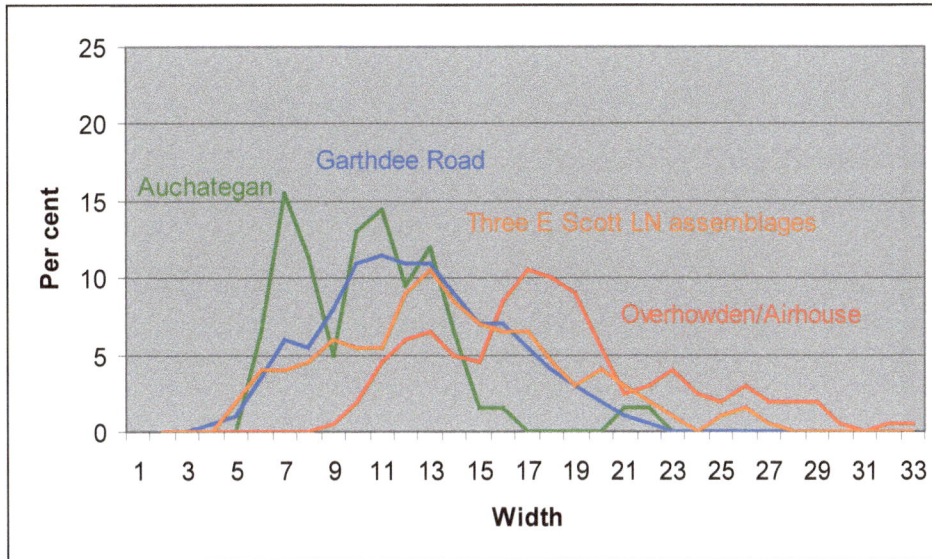

Fig. 31. The blade width of a series of Scottish blade assemblages.

the following later Bronze Age period being char-acterized by the production of squat flakes (Ballin 2002a).

It has been established in other parts of North-West Europe that the average blade width of individual prehistoric industries constitutes a useful dating tool (Denmark: Andersen 1982; Southern Norway: Ballin 2004a, 420), and in Britain it has been commonly known for most of a century that, for example, it is possible to subdivide the Mesolithic period into an early broad-blade period and a later narrow-blade period (eg, Mellars 1974). In connection with the author's daily work as a lithics specialist in Scotland and, not least, a series of substantial projects, such as The Pitchstone Project (Ballin 2009) and the present project, it has become clear that it is also possible to subdivide the Scottish Neolithic period along these lines, with blades developing from narrow towards broad blades. It is an important point in connection with the use of average blade width as a dating tool that unmixed, statistically sound blade assemblages tend to produce a bell-shaped curve, where mixed assemblages tend to have more than one peak (cf. the analysis of the finds from the Glentaggart chert assemblage from South Lanarkshire; Ballin & Johnson 2005, 83-4)

Fig. 31 shows a series of Scottish blade assemblages which may provide an impression of the general trend in Scotland. It should be borne in mind, that this is not in any way a final result, as many more assemblages need to be analysed to produce an authoritative metric checklist for dating Scottish blade assemblages. The blades from Auchategan in Argyll & Bute form an obvious double-peaked curve (av. blade widths: 7 mm / 10-13 mm; Table 14), and it was argued in the Auchategan publication (Ballin 2006) that this assemblage is likely to represent two main visits to the site in the Early Neolithic period. The analysis of the Scottish pitchstone assemblages showed that the very

earliest part of the Early Neolithic period is characterized by blades as narrow as typical Late Mesolithic blades, and that blades start growing substantially broader soon after the Mesolithic/Neolithic transition.

Auchategan	7 mm / 10-13 mm
Garthdee Road	10-13 mm
LN E Scott average	13 mm
Overhowden/Airhouse	13 mm / 18 mm

Table 14. The average blade width of a number of Scottish Neolithic assemblages.

The blades from Garthdee Road in Aberdeen (Ballin forthcoming g) form a regular bell-shaped curve, suggesting that this assemblage may have been deposited within a very short period. The peak of this curve (av. blade width 10-13 mm) corresponds roughly to the second peak at Auchategan, and the second visit to the Auchategan site may be approximately contemporary with the main settlement at Garthdee Road. Radiocarbon dates from Garthdee Road (Sheridan 2007, 480) indicates a date around 5000-4900 BP (calibration of the earliest and latest dates by the use of the programme OxCal 4.1 provided the following range [95.4% certainty]: 3943-3710 to 3775-3646 cal BC [SUERC-8617 and -8608]), supporting the trends indicated by the Scottish Pitchstone Project.

A series of numerically relatively small Late Neolithic blade assemblages (East Lochside, Midmill and Stoneyhill from Angus and Aberdeenshire; Johnson & Ballin 2006; Ballin forthcoming h; Suddaby & Ballin forthcoming) were combined to obtain a statistically acceptable population. This approach has it pitfalls and may explain why this curve is so broad. The curve's peak is at 13 mm, slightly to the right of the peak of the Garthdee Road blade assemblage. It should be noted that, although the Midmill assemblage includes some Grooved Ware period blades, the vast majority of the blades from East Lochside and Stoneyhill were associated with Impressed Ware.

An attempt to produce two separate curves for the blades from Airhouse and Overhowden proved unfruitful, as the latter assemblage is too numerically small to be statistically reliable: the blade assemblage from Airhouse includes 75 pieces, whereas the blade assemblage from Overhowden only includes 13 pieces. It was therefore decided to combine the blades from the two assemblages. The blades from Airhouse/Overhowden form a clearly dichotomous curve, with one set of blades having an average width of 13 mm and another with an average width of 18 mm. The fact that one of these peaks (13 mm) corresponds approximately to the peak of the three Late Neolithic East

of Scotland assemblages makes it tempting to suggest that this peak represents the Airhouse/Overhowden Impressed Ware period blades and that the peak further to the right (18 mm) may represent this collection's Grooved Ware period blades.

However, it should be borne in mind, that the picture presented above could have been influenced by the different raw material situations in the various Scottish regions (Argyll & Bute, East of Scotland, and the Scottish Borders), where the latter region may have had much easier access to supplies of Yorkshire flint. This could mean that blades from the Scottish Borders are generally somewhat broader than blades from more northerly regions. Nevertheless, 31 and Table 14 clearly define the bulk of the Airhouse/Overhowden finds as Late Neolithic.

3. FUNCTIONAL CHARACTERIZATION OF THE AIRHOUSE AND OVERHOWDEN SITES – COMPARATIVE ANALYSIS

3.1 Brief summary of the Airhouse/Overhowden assemblage

Before the Airhouse/Overhowden assemblage is compared with other Late Neolithic assemblages from Scotland and the British Isles, it is essential to briefly summarize the lithic finds from those two sites in terms of basic composition, raw material preferences, typological composition, applied technological approaches and dating.

3.1.1 Basic composition

Usually, the first step of assemblage characterization is dealing with the collection's basic elements, that is, its total numerical size, and its main artefact categories (numbers of debitage, cores and tools).

In total, 667 lithic artefacts were recovered from the two sites, with the Airhouse collection numbering 558 pieces and the Overhowden assemblage 109. The combined assemblage includes practically no debitage (21 pieces or 3%), whereas 3 Levallois-like cores were retrieved (approximately 0.5%), as well as 643 tools (c. 96%). Basically, almost all of the finds from the two locations are implements.

Unless no primary reduction took place at Airhouse and Overhowden, this composition must reflect selective processes of recovery. The fact that most of the tools show medium-grade to heavy use-wear makes absence of primary reduction appear implausible. As tools were being worn, some would have required repair and others replacement, and a complete lack of primary knapping at the two sites is unlikely – no matter which potentially specialized functions the sites fulfilled in Late Neolithic society. If this premise is accepted, the combined collection must have been exposed to selective processes in the field as well as after collection.

It is a well-known fact that fieldwalking usually results in the recovery of more large pieces than small pieces, for obvious reasons, and it is also generally accepted that many fieldwalkers have a tendency to pick more regular and 'nice' pieces than irregular, more 'natural-looking' pieces (cf. Schofield 2000). Selection after collection is suggested by the almost complete absence of unmodified blanks and cores. If it is accepted that some primary knapping may have taken place at the two locations, it is highly unlikely that only tools would have been recovered in the field, as many blanks are also regular (for example Late Neolithic macroblades), and it is assumed that a collection of almost exclusively tools must have been prepared for the

Scottish National Museum prior to the exchange between finder and museum. The three Levallois-like cores may have been included in the assemblage, as such pieces occasionally look like small unpolished axeheads or 'celts' (Moore 1963, 192).

To allow comparison with other (usually excavated) Late Neolithic assemblages – most of which would not have been exposed to similar selective processes – it is therefore important that an attempt is made at estimating the original numerical size of the assemblage. As shown in Fig. 32, there is a clear correlation between an excavated collection's tool ratio and its status as sieved or unsieved, with sieved assemblages usually having tool ratios between c. 0.5-4% and unsieved ones between c. 5-10% (in both cases, with some deviating assemblages/ratios). This suggests that, if the two sites had been excavated, and the soil wet-sieved, the combined assemblage would have had an original numerical size of c. 16,650-133,200 (for comparison with unsieved assemblages, the numbers would be c. 6,660-13,320). If the sites had had special functions in the local Late Neolithic assemblage, with less primary knapping taking place, these numbers might have been somewhat smaller, but the combined Airhouse/ Overhowden assemblage would still have been substantial.

3.1.2 Raw material preferences

The combined assemblage is predominantly in flint (95-98%), and the collection's small amounts of chert appear mainly to be associated with its Early Neolithic and Early Bronze Age elements. Although some local Scottish flint was recovered (c. 6%), most of the finds are in grey and dark-brown exotic flint. The exotic nature of the flint is suggested by the soft cortex of several pieces (3%).

The grey flints are mostly marbled (75%), and to a degree small-dotted (21%), whereas the dark-brown flints are mostly homogeneous (75%), and to a lesser extent marbled (20%). The colours and patterning of the flints are consistent with the variation encountered in Yorkshire flint, and it is therefore assumed that almost all of the flint recovered from Airhouse and Overhowden was procured from sources in the greater Yorkshire area.

3.1.3 Typological composition

The general composition of the tools is shown in Table 2, with Late Neolithic arrowheads dominating (38%), closely followed by scrapers (28%). Earlier and later arrowheads make up 9%, and knives 7%. Other important tool forms are polished-edge implements, piercers, strike-a-lights,

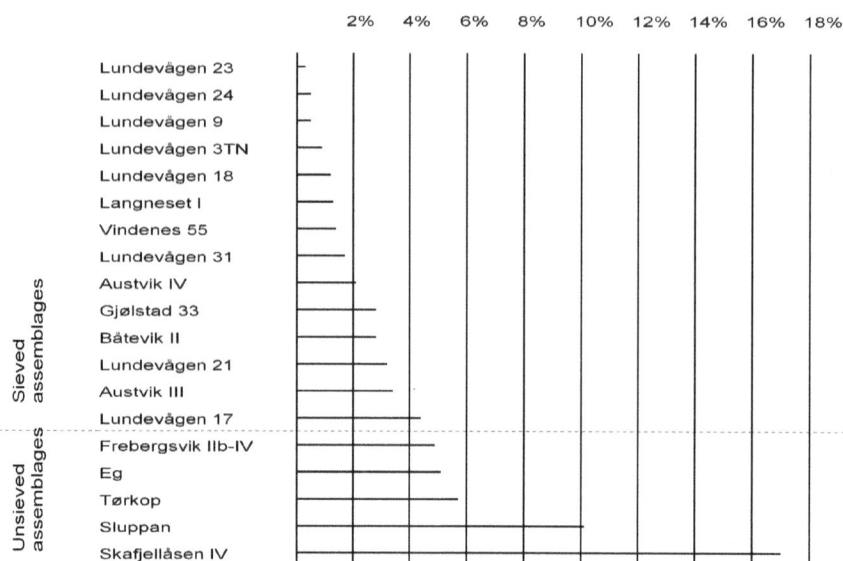

Fig. 32. Tool ratios of some sieved and unsieved assemblages from southern Norway (Ballin 1999b)

serrated pieces/saws, and combined tools, which amount to 1-3% each. The finds also include a solitary intact edge-polished adzehead.

In Chapter 2.3.1, it was argued that the 242 Late Neolithic arrowheads are distributed across three main types, namely chisel-shaped arrowheads (49%), oblique arrowheads (14%), and a deviating form (24%). Use-wear suggests that chisel-shaped arrowheads were mounted as transverse arrowheads, whereas the latter two forms were mounted as tipped forms. In terms of raw material, chisel-shaped pieces are mainly in grey flint, oblique arrowheads in dark-brown flint, whereas the deviating group forms a hybrid category. In addition, some pieces were defined as rough-outs (five pieces), and some were too fragmented for detailed classification (26 pieces). Furthermore, a small number of oblique and deviating forms were defined as bifacial (20 pieces, nine of which also had full modification of the cutting-edges) or ripple-flaked (four pieces).

Earlier and later arrowheads are leaf-shaped and barbed-and-tanged points, which are approximately equally numerous (35 and 26 pieces, respectively). As mentioned above, these categories include more chert objects than the Late Neolithic arrowheads (34% and 11%, respectively, against 0.5%). Both categories include substantial proportions of Yorkshire flint (approximately 68% and 82% of the respective groups' flint specimens). A total of 15% of the leaf-shaped forms are kite-shaped, with most of the remaining ones being small, squat teardrop-shaped or double-pointed pieces. All barbed-and-tanged points belong to one of the three Sutton categories, with 'fancy' pieces being absent.

A single edge-polished adzehead belongs to a relatively plain sub-form with a thin bifacial polished band along the working-edge. With its straight, tapering lateral sides it differs from the more accomplished Late Neolithic axeheads and adzeheads of Seamer/Duggleby Type.

The collection's knives are predominantly scale-flaked (35 pieces) and plano-convex (4 pieces) forms, supplemented by one backed knife, one discoidal knife, and one polished-edge knife. Single-edged as well as double-edged variants are represented. The discoidal knife and the polished-edge knife were both modified by a combination of invasive retouch and polish. Use-wear analysis (carried out by Dr Randy Donahue, Bradford University) of scale-flaked knives with macroscopically visible gloss showed that this category (and probably also the related plano-convex knives) were used for cutting/sickling grasses or cereals.

The large scraper group (179 pieces) are distributed across a variety of morphological sub-types, with short end-scrapers (113 pieces) and side-scrapers (including side-/end-scrapers and double-/side-scrapers: 41 pieces) being the most numerous forms. In addition, the scrapers include eight discoidal scrapers, seven blade-scrapers, six double-scrapers, one concave scraper, and three indeterminate scraper-edge fragments. Many scrapers have blunted lateral edges, and most show distinct, frequently heavy, use-wear.

Twenty-one polished-edge implements form a distinct part of the finds from Airhouse/Overhowden. Although the group includes two side-scrapers and two edge-retouched pieces with polished edges, most were in their origin end-scrapers. The polished areas range from slightly abraded protruding areas along the tools' working-edges to completely rounded working-edges. Although use-wear analysis of three pieces by Dr Donahue (Bradford University) determined that these implements had been used to process dry hide, the exact function of the category is presently uncertain. Traditional scraping is out of the question, as this form of work would require sharp working-edges.

Eight strike-a-lights form an equally distinct part of the collection. They are generally based on robust, elongated blanks, and they have either one or two abraded terminals. Two pieces are recycled tools and based on a scale-flaked knife and an end-scraper, respectively. With seventeen pieces, combined tools form a relatively numerous category. They are all scale-flaked or plano-convex knives which have been combined either with a scraper-edge or with a piercer tip (nine and six pieces, respectively). One piece is combined with the working-end of a strike-a-light, and one with a polished edge.

The collection's eleven piercers are in most cases based on elongated blanks, and they usually have distal tips, formed by merging two lateral retouched areas. A small number of deviating forms have their tips at suitable corners or on suitable lateral edges. Serrated pieces and saws – that is, implements with more or less fine serration – amount to five pieces. Two serrated pieces and three saws were recovered from the two sites. Although pieces with two opposed serrated edges are known, the ones from Airhouse/Overhowden are all single-edged pieces, occasionally with an opposed blunted edge.

Other tools include Neolithic/Bronze Age truncated (two), notched (two), bifacial (two), and variously retouched pieces (48), as well as one early prehistoric burin and one post-Medieval gunflint.

3.1.4 Technological approaches

In the Late Neolithic period, the Airhouse/Overhowden lithic industry was based almost entirely on imported Yorkshire flint, supplemented by minuscule amounts of local Scottish raw materials. Although some blanks are likely to have been struck from traditional platform cores (none of which formed part of the collection originally offered to National Museums Scotland), the attributes of the blanks indicate that most were detached from Levallois-like cores (three of which had been retained by the original collector and gifted to National Museums Scotland). Each tool category included between c. 10% and 30% pieces with finely faceted platform remnants (Table 11), and if fragmentation (eg, the absence of a proximal end) and other biasing factors are taken into account, this ratio would originally have been much higher. The low ratio of finely faceted pieces in the PTD category (2%) is probably due to the fact that most of them had their butts altered as part of the secondary modification of these pieces.

The relative proportions of primary, secondary and tertiary pieces indicate that the Levallois-like cores were carefully decorticated before blank production commenced. Similarities between the collection's flake and blade blanks (in both cases, 70% are tertiary pieces) is perceived as evidence that the industry aimed at the simultaneous production of broad flake blanks and slender blade blanks from the same Levallois-like cores. As shown by Table 12, the tools include 88 blade blanks (or 25% of all tool blanks), most of which (90%) are hard-percussion blades. It is thought that a level of blank specialization took place at Airhouse/Overhowden, in the sense that it was attempted to produce certain blanks for certain tool forms. Arrowheads and tools meant for heavy-duty rubbing or striking (such as scrapers, polished-edge implements and strike-a-lights) are predominantly based on flakes, whereas cutting implements (knives, serrated pieces and saws) are mostly based on blades.

Secondary modification of the tool blanks was carried out in a number of different ways, such as by removing, thinning or narrowing the bulbar end, probably to facilitate hafting. The working-edge of the implements was formed either by traditional edge-retouch (resulting in a relatively steep edge; eg, most scrapers, piercers) or invasive retouch (resulting in a relatively acute edge; eg, most arrowheads, knives). Two tool forms were shaped partly by scale-flaking and partly by polish, namely the polished-edge implements and the discoidal and polished-edge knives. It is uncertain whether the polish of the former represents actual modification or use-wear. The combination of different working-edges on the same tool blank is a characteristic element of this industry, but it is uncertain whether this represents a mental template (ie, this was how the pieces were shaped from the out-set, following a form of 'Swiss army knife' principle) or whether this is a form of recycling (ie, where one working-edge was added at a later stage, when the primary working-edge had been exhausted). The fact that no form of working-edge seems to be more worn than any other supports the former interpretation.

3.1.5 Dating

The lithic finds from Airhouse and Overhowden (eg, the relative proportions of the main diagnostic arrowhead types: leaf-shaped forms, PTDs, and barbed-and-tanged forms) indicate that probably about 80% of the combined assemblage is Late Neolithic, and that the Late Neolithic finds cover earlier and later stages of this general period.

A general Late Neolithic date is suggested by the dominance of Yorkshire flint, which is usually associated with this period. The collection's Early Neolithic and Bronze Age diagnostic artefacts include notably higher proportions of non-flint (mainly local chert), as well as notably higher proportions of non-Yorkshire flint (ie, local pebble flint), than its typical Late Neolithic artefacts.

Amongst the Late Neolithic artefacts, simpler (and earlier) PTDs are predominantly in grey exotic flint, whereas more sophisticated (and later) PTDs are predominantly in dark-brown exotic flint.

In addition to the PTDs, the assemblage includes several other tool types which support a mostly Late Neolithic date, such as one edge-ground adzehead, one discoidal knife, one polished-edge knife, polished-edge implements, blade-based strike-a-lights, and combined tools. Some of these types are strictly diagnostic, like for example discoidal knives (mainly Grooved Ware contexts) and polished-edge knives (mainly Impressed Ware contexts), whereas others are diagnostic as a result of their specific form, their high numbers, or their technological attributes.

The Late Neolithic majority of the collection is also dated by its specific technological attributes. This includes attributes characteristic of the strictly Late Neolithic Levallois-like approach (first and foremost the blanks' finely faceted platform remnants, but also the high number of hard-percussion blades). In comparison, most Early Neolithic blades were detached by soft percussion, and Bronze Age assemblages do not include *proper* blade blanks. The average width of the blades from Airhouse/Overhowden also support a generally Late Neolithic date, but this relative dating method needs more research before it can be used with full confidence (more well-dated single-occupation assemblages from this period need to be made available for attribute analysis).

3.2 Definition of assemblages from different Late Neolithic site types

In the introduction of Chapter 1.5, it was emphasized that the purpose of that chapter was not to list all Late Neolithic sites from Britain or all British papers in which Late Neolithic lithics have been discussed, but to highlight key achievements on the way towards expanding our understanding of Late Neolithic lithics. In the same way, the purpose of the present chapter is not to list or discuss all Late Neolithic assemblages from Britain, assigned to the various site categories below but, by the use of carefully selected cases, to define which Late Neolithic site types are generally characterized by which lithic assemblages. It will be attempted to apply Scottish assemblages to the extent this is possible.

The following site types were defined: 1) extraction sites (procurement sites, quarries/mines, pebble sources); 2) domestic sites; 3) settlements functionally linked to ritual sites; 4) ritual sites (henges, stone circles, standing stones, rock art sites); and 5) burials.

3.2.1 Assemblages from extraction sites

In most cases, extraction sites are associated with other activities than the quarrying or collection of raw materials. These activities include 1) the breaking up of quarried material into large blocks (the tailing pile), 2) the breaking down of these blocks for transport (the ore dressing, milling, or transition area), and 3) the reduction of smaller ('quartered') blocks into core rough-outs and preforms as well as, in some cases, final tools (the lithic reduction site) (Schneiderman-Fox & Pappalardo 1996; also Ballin 2004b).

These three types of areas are usually located at increasing distances to the actual point of extraction (quarries/collection fields), where areas associated with the crudest lithic material are found closest to this point and areas associated with finer lithic material further away. The present chapter is not concerned with the actual extraction or collection processes, but only with the assemblages associated with these sites.

In Britain, Late Neolithic extraction sites are relatively common (eg, Barber *et al.* 1999, Fig. 1.2), but only a small number of these have been presented and discussed in detail. In the present chapter, focus is on the finds from Grimes Graves in Norfolk (Saville 1981), Den of Boddam/Skelmuir Hill in Aberdeenshire (Saville 1995; 2005; 2006; 2008), and South Landing in Yorkshire (Durden 1995; Gardiner 2008, 240). These three sites represent extraction based on the quarrying of primary outcrops (bedrock sources: Grimes Graves), the quarrying of secondary outcrops (gravel sources: Boddam/Skelmuir Hill), and the collection of pebbles and cobbles eroding out of the till (South Landing).

The characterization of the Late Neolithic finds from the 1971 shaft at Grimes Graves, and areas around the shaft (particularly Trenches 3-6, Layer 3), showed a number of interesting trends (Saville 1981). The finds generally include:

- A high number of waste flakes, but few cores and implements (ibid., 32, 35); the waste flakes generally amount to *c.* 97-98%, with cores amounting to 0.2-0.7% and tools 1.2-2.5%.
- A low number of core rejuvenation flakes and finely faceted blanks (ibid., 41); the core rejuvenation flakes are mostly flakes from the adjustment of platforms, but the present author believes that Saville's '... *triangular sectioned flakes struck obliquely to the platform to rejuvenate the platform edge*' may actually be crested pieces, or guide ridges;
- A low number of finely faceted pieces (ibid., 41); across the trenches, the faceted butt ratios varied between 4-10%, with finely faceted platform remnants (Saville's faceted butts *sensu stricto*) forming a relatively small proportion of those;
- A relatively high ratio of tertiary blanks (*c.* 70%) (ibid., 40);
- A relatively high blade ratio, or lamellar index (*c.* 20%) (ibid., 43); and

- A very limited tool spectrum (ibid., 68); the tools include one PTD, four picks, seven axes, two discoidal knives, 12 scrapers, 27 points, 37 cutting flakes, 26 utilized blades, and a small number of other implement forms.

In his attempt to explain these trends, Saville (ibid., 68) states that there is no evidence to support the view that the assemblage from the Late Neolithic knapping floor from the 1971 shaft at Grimes Graves is an assemblage produced by the specialized manufacture of one tool form, such as axes (or for that matter discoidal knives; cf. Gardiner 2008, 239), as seems to have been the case at other flint mines in southern England (eg, Blackpatch/Church Hill [axes] and Cissbury [blades and knives]; Russell 2000, 118).

The obviously skewed core:waste ratios from Trenches 3 and 4 (1:174 and 1:646) is difficult to explain, but some spent cores may have been removed from the knapping floor by 'tossing', or they may have been carried away as part of general site maintenance or clearance (Binford 1983, 189). It is also quite likely that one of the aims of the Late Neolithic quarriers was to produce rough-out Levallois-like cores for distribution to other parts of the region (or further afield), which would explain the low number of crested pieces (struck from the core at the beginning of blank production proper) and finely faceted blanks (most likely, fine faceting was carried out immediately prior to the onset of blank production). However, the high number of tertiary blanks, as well as true blades, indicates that some primary production took place at the site, and it is possible that the main aim of the Trench 3 and 4 quarriers and knappers was to produce not only rough cores for export, but also bundles of unmodified flakes and blades.

In his comparison between the Late Neolithic and Middle Bronze Age assemblages at the 1971 shaft, Saville (1981, 68) emphasizes that '... *the Middle Bronze Age assemblage is from a classic occupation deposit with pottery, bone, calcined flint, charcoal, etc., whereas the Late Neolithic deposit is fundamentally a chipping floor without non-lithic associations*'. This explains the limited tool spectrum at the Late Neolithic site, where a large proportion of the implements may have been associated with mining activities (eg, picks and points), whereas others may have been associated with the general subsistence of the quarriers/knappers ('... *some domestic implements for immediate use*'; ibid., 70), explaining the expedient character of some of the finds (eg, the cutting flakes and utilized blades).

In summary, the lithic evidence from the 1971 shaft seems to suggest that, although some axe rough-outs and preforms of discoidal knives were produced (ibid., 70), the main aim of the quarriers and knappers may have been to extract flint for the production of rough cores and unmodified blanks for exchange (exchange is here, and in the following text, defined as in Renfrew (1977, 72), that is '... *in the case of some distributions it is not established*

that the goods changed hands at all; [exchange] in this case implies procurement of materials from a distance, by whatever mechanism').

Although the quarrying process at Den of Boddam and Skelmuir Hill was different to that experienced at Grimes Graves (due to the different geological settings), the lithic material indicates that the same post-extraction processes took place. Like at Grimes Graves, the lithics (generally perceived to be of Late Neolithic date; Saville 2008, 5) seem to represent knapping floors rather than actual settlement, and hearths, postholes, pottery and other elements of Late Neolithic material culture were entirely absent (Saville 1995, 363). Where at Grimes Graves the Late Neolithic assemblage included some formal and expedient tools, the only implements found at the Aberdeenshire quarrying complex are occasional *ad hoc* tool forms (Saville 2008, 8). The production apparently aimed at producing mostly Levallois-like cores for export out of the site, and possibly also raw tool blanks. This process was carried out by 1) splitting nodules by the application of bipolar technique, and 2) shaping the cores, and detaching tool blanks, by the application of hard percussion (Saville 1995, 363; 2005, 7; 2006, 450; 2008, 7). In general, the lithic finds from Den of Boddam and Skelmuir Hill only include knapping tools (such as quartzite hammers and anvils), cores (mainly Levallois-like forms), and unmodified waste and tool blanks.

Durdens (1995) paper on possible lithic specialization in Late Neolithic Yorkshire, describes two very different sites, South Landing and North Dale. The former may be an extraction site, where flint collected from the cliffs and beaches at Flamborough Head was gathered and tested, and where cores (many of which belong to the Levallois-like category) and raw tool blanks were being manufactured for export to inland sites in the region and further afield (ibid., 417, 423). In contrast, the assemblage from the inland site North Dale includes not only debitage and cores (many of which are Levallois-like), but also substantial numbers of tools (ibid. 423). Many of the implements from North Dale belong to categories frequently referred to as prestige goods, such as a Seamer type axe, discoidal knives, as well as ripple-flaked and polished oblique arrowheads (ibid., 411) (also see account in Gardiner 2008, 240).

Assemblages from Late Neolithic extraction sites are characterized mainly by restricted formal variation, and they are summarized in Chapter 3.3.

3.2.2 Assemblages from domestic settlements

In positive terms, domestic sites are characterized by features such as dwellings, hearths, fences and other enclosures (like the Storey's Bar 'cattle droves'), rubbish pits and middens, as well as (frequently large amounts of) domestic pottery (all these elements are not necessarily present at each site). In negative terms, domestic sites are defined by the absence of extraction shafts or pits, as well as ritual features and burials. A number of English assemblages were compared by Healy (1985, 192), and as she states: '*Lack of common classification [principles] hampers the comparison of the retouched components of industries examined by different individuals. For this reason, only the retouched pieces of the four industries examined by the author are compared in detail*'. The assemblages dealt with by Healy are: Tye Field, Essex (Healy 1985); Storey's Bar Road, Cambridgeshire (Pryor 1978); Lion Point, Essex (Wilson *et al.* 1971); Honington, Norfolk (Fell 1952); Creeting St Mary, Suffolk (Wainwright & Longworth 1971, 284); and Hunstanton, Norfolk (Healy 1993). Scottish assemblages included in this section are East Lochside, Angus (Ballin 2005; Johnson & Ballin 2006); Stoneyhill Area 1/Grid J, Aberdeenshire (Suddaby & Ballin forthcoming); and Pool, Orkney (Finlayson 2007). The latter material was included partly to allow comparison with the assemblage from Barnhouse, also Orkney (below).

The raw material used on the English sites appears to be mostly local material (eg, Healy 1985, 182, 194; 1993, 28). However, without surviving cortex, flint artefacts are notoriously difficult to provenance, and any attempt at provenancing English flint assemblages is characterized by a relatively high level of uncertainty. The Scottish material is considerably easier to provenance, even on colour and patterning alone, and there is little doubt that the assemblages from East Lochside (Ballin 2005) and Pool (inspected at Orkney Museum 2009) include small amounts of Yorkshire flint (at East Lochside estimated at 4%). The assemblage from Stoneyhill Area 1/Grid J is probably entirely in Buchan Ridge flint, as the settlement is situated on top of the Buchan Ridge Gravels (Suddaby & Ballin forthcoming).

Generally, the assemblages include large sub-assemblages of waste flakes and unmodified blanks. Healy's comparison does not reveal the relative proportions of debitage:cores:tools for all the sites – these values are given for Tye Field: 81:3:16% (1,450 pieces of debitage of 1,794 flints) – but examination of the original site reports shows that this is the case. At Honington, for example, flakes amount to 10,226 pieces (82% of 12,410 pieces); at Hunstanton, flakes, blades and irregular waste amount to 1,194 pieces (80% of 1,494 flints); and at Storey's Bar Road (Divisions 1-9), these categories make up 2,091 pieces (68% of 3,076 flints).

The Scottish sites yielded similar proportions of lithic waste and unmodified blanks. At East Lochside, 479 pieces were defined as debitage (84% of 570 lithics); at Stoneyhill Area 1/Grid J, this category numbered 688 pieces (81% of 850 lithics); and at Pool these artefacts amounted to 9,325 pieces (97% of 9,618 lithics). It is thought that the varying percentages mostly represent differences in terms of archaeological methodologies (eg, excavation techniques, sieving/not sieving, etc.), and applied prehistoric reduction techniques (platform technique and bipolar technique, for

example, create different volumes of waste per finished tool; Ballin 1999a), rather than prehistoric activity-based differences. The main point at this stage of the comparison, is that all these assemblages include much primary lithic waste. All the above assemblages embrace varying numbers of true blades (eg, Healy 1985, 193), and in general the bulk of the debitage was created by the application of hard percussion (at Pool also bipolar technique), with soft-percussion blanks being more or less absent from the Late Neolithic contexts.

Another well-represented artefact group at domestic Late Neolithic sites is cores. As mentioned above, the Tye Field assemblage includes 3% cores (50 pieces), and the other assemblages compared by Healy (ibid.) include between 40 and 70 cores (Healy's account [ibid., Table 12] does not match the numbers given in the primary publications: cores from Honington, for example, only make up seven pieces, although Fell's [1952, 43] account gives the number 1,877, corresponding to 15%; the specimens in Healy's table must represent unspecified selection). In the primary publications, the Hunstanton cores amount to 103 pieces, or 7%, and the Storey's Bar Road assemblage has 41 cores, or 1%. The core ratios for the above-mentioned Scottish assemblages (East Lochside, Stoneyhill Area 1/Grid J and Pool) are 7%, 5%, and 6%, respectively.

Generally, the core ratio of Late Neolithic domestic assemblages seems to be approximately 5-7%, with the assemblages from Honington (whether one accepts Healy's or Fell's numbers) and Storey's Bar Road deviating from the norm (1%/15% and 1%, respectively). Due to the different figures given for the Honington cores, it is not possible to determine why (or whether?) the core ratio of this assemblage deviates. The low number of cores (and the relatively low debitage ratio/high tool ratio) of the material from Storey's Bar Road may be due to usable cores having been removed from the site when people left the site in connection with seasonal movements/transhumance (this is supported by the 'flimsy' character of dwellings suggested by Pryor [1978, 158]). Levallois-like cores (or, in the older literature, discoidal or keeled cores), are common elements of, or dominates, all the core assemblages.

Healy's (1985, 195) comparison of the tools recovered from Tye Field, Honington, Creeting St Mary, and Hunstanton, shows some similarities between the assemblages, but also many differences. Scrapers and simple edge-retouched pieces dominate all four assemblages substantially, but the proportions of other important tool categories vary: PTDs are relatively common at Tye Field and Honington, but fairly rare at Creeting St Mary and Hunstanton; piercers are relatively common at Creeting St Mary, but virtually absent at Hunstanton (apart from a small number of spurred implements); and serrated pieces are common at Honington, Creeting St Mary and Hunstanton, but rare at Tye Field. It should be noted that: scale-flaked knives are present at Tye Field, but absent from the other three assemblages; that discoidal knives and strike-a-lights (ie, fabricators) are present in some of the assemblages, but generally not common; and that polished axeheads, polished-edge knives, polished-edge implements and sophisticated combined tools are absent from all assemblages (although Healy's Fig. 17.F24 seems to portray a polished-edge implement [scraper]).

There is a discrepancy between Healy's implement account (ibid., 195), which lists 'flakes from polished implements' (probably flakes from axeheads) at Tye Field and Hunstanton, and discoidal knives at Tye Field, Creeting St Mary and Hunstanton, and that of Wainwright & Longworth (1971, 256), which lists 'implements with polished edges' at Tye Field, Creeting St Mary and Honington, and discoidal knives at Tye Field only. Most likely, some of Wainwright & Longworths's 'implements with polished edges' are discoidal knives, and some may be flakes detached from cannibalized polished flint axeheads. Apparently, polished flint axeheads were rarely deposited intact on Late Neolithic domestic sites, but the cannibalization (ie, recycling) of polished axeheads did occur on those sites.

At Storey's Bar Road (Pryor 1978, 137), scrapers and arrowheads dominate the implement category heavily (76% and 14%, respectively), and simple edge-retouched forms are rare. The relative rarity of simple edge-retouched (ie, expedient) forms at this settlement may reflect the special character of the site, where many tools may have been brought onto the site in finished form, due to the practice of some form of transhumance (as discussed above, in connection with the discussion of the relative rarity of cores at Storey's Bar Road).

The Scottish assemblages are generally characterized by the presence of relatively plain tool forms, and in all cases scrapers dominate markedly. The East Lochside collection include 35% scrapers, Stoneyhill Area 1/Grid J 21%, and Pool 45%. All three assemblages also include substantial numbers of simple edge-retouched forms (39%, 58%, and 27%, respectively). At East Lochside, PTDs are relatively common (12%), whereas they are 'present' at the other two Late Neolithic sites (c. 2% and <1%, respectively). The Pool assemblage includes one possible strike-a-light (fabricator) and one scale-flaked knife, but none of the assemblages embraces polished axeheads, discoidal/polished-edge knives, polished-edge implements (a polished tool at Pool is likely to be an implement based on a flake from a cannibalized polished axe), or combined tools.

As described above, the assemblages differ considerably in terms of their general composition – for example, which implements dominate the tools – but it is thought that this variation may reflect economical differences: the dominance of scrapers, for example, may reflect an element of animal husbandry (cattle?); arrowheads (in contexts like these) may reflect archery/hunting; and serrated pieces

may indicate non-subsistence related activities, such as the processing of fibres, but not cutting cereals (Juel Jensen 1994, 68). The limited use-wear analysis of scale-flaked knives carried out in connection with the present project seems to indicate that Late Neolithic sickling of cereals may mainly have been carried out by scale-flaked knives (Chapter 2.3.2) – which are relatively rare on British Late Neolithic domestic sites.

Characteristic elements of assemblages from Late Neolithic domestic sites are summarized in Chapter 3.3.

3.2.3 Assemblages from settlements functionally linked to ritual sites

This category includes assemblages recovered *at relatively short distances from* ritual sites, like for example henges, but *not material recovered within or beneath them*, even though the finds may represent activities taking place in connection with, for instance, the erection of the monuments (and thereby technically 'functionally linked' to those). The latter finds are dealt with in connection with the discussion of the full assemblages from ritual sites (3.2.4).

Assemblages belonging to the present category are still relatively rare, although some are expected to 'materialize' as part of the post-excavation work carried out on finds from the investigation of the landscapes surrounding monuments like Thornborough in Yorkshire and Stonehenge in Withshire. At the present moment, no detailed accounts of the lithic finds from these projects have been published, but it has been suggested that some of the finds from the immediate vicinity of large henges, or from slightly further afield, may have been associated either with the building of the monuments, or with actual rituals (pilgrimage?) at the henges (Harding 2000, 38; 2003, 62; Chan 2009). At Thornborough, substantial surface collections of flint have been recovered *c.* half a kilometre to one kilometre from the three henges, but few flint artefacts were found in or immediately around them (Harding 2003, Fig. 46).

At present, the best representatives of this assemblage category are two collections from Orkney, namely Barnhouse (Middleton 2005) and Ness of Brodgar (examined by the author at orkney College 2010; also Wickham-Jones in prep.), which were recovered from two Late Neolithic settlements near two impressive ritual monuments, Stones of Stenness and Ring of Brodgar.

Unfortunately, the published assemblage from Barnhouse is in a format (Middleton 2005, 299) that makes it very difficult to obtain a detailed overview of the finds, but it is obvious that scrapers and simple edge-retouched forms are the two most common categories. The report text and its illustrations indicate that this assemblage includes notably more scale-flaked knives, and flakes from cannibalized polished axeheads (the report's polished-edge implements are probably all flakes from axeheads) than assemblages from ordinary domestic sites, with some piercers and PTDs being present. As described in Chapter 3.2.2, the domestic Pool assemblage, also from Orkney, includes practically no 'fancy' elements.

The author's inspection of the Barnhouse flints at Orkney Museum showed that this collection contains substantially more Yorkshire flint than, for example, the contemporary assemblage from the domestic site of Pool and, as a consequence, the artefacts at the former site are generally larger than those of the latter. The finds from Barnhouse also include relatively large numbers of pitchstone artefacts (Ballin forthcoming b), imported from Arran, where the Pool collection includes none.

The lithic finds from the Ness of Brodgar site (excavations still ongoing, 2010) is numerically smaller than the collection from Barnhouse (currently *c.* 500 pieces against *c.* 1,600 pieces), but its composition is equally interesting. The author's summary examination showed that: possibly about 50% of the flint is Yorkshire flint, and there are good hard-hammer blades, chisel-shaped arrowheads, many scale-flaked knives, strike-a-lights, and scrapers. Several flakes and knives were recovered as caches or clusters. Due to the lack of a formal artefact list in the Barnhouse report, it has not been able to calculate the tool ratio of that material.

Apart from their closeness to Orkney's central ritual monuments, the two sites, Barnhouse and Ness of Brodgar, are also characterized by the presence of Skara Brae type houses (Foster 2006) of above-average sizes (where for example Pool included more modest houses), and sizeable pottery assemblages (Grooved Ware).

One assemblage which may belong to this category is that of Doon Hill, East Lothian. The site was excavated by Hope-Taylor between 1964 and 1966 , who showed that two timber halls had stood successively on the site, surrounded by a polygonal palisade. In the northern part of the area encircled by the palisade, a small square structure was discovered, which may have been associated with a cremation cemetery.

Since the site's excavation, the dates of the various features have been discussed. The smaller of the two halls was built after the greater hall had been destroyed by fire. Until recently, consensus was that both buildings were Dark Age structures, and that the lithic finds are residual (Hope-Taylor 1980), but it has also been suggested (Scott 1989, 272) that the larger building may actually belong to the growing list of Early Neolithic timber halls (cf. Sheridan 2007, 445).

Although it is always possible to discuss whether finds from postholes and trenches are contemporary with these features, or whether they entered the features with the back-fill and thereby pre-date the features (by decades,

centuries or millennia), the dichotomous nature of the find distribution suggests that the finds and the features may actually be contemporary: Early Neolithic types and technological attributes, as well as a raw material (Arran pitchstone) generally exchanged during the first half of the Early Neolithic period, are associated with the site's greater hall, and Late Neolithic types and technological attributes, as well as a raw material (Yorkshire flint) generally exchanged during the Impressed Ware and Grooved Ware periods, are associated with the palisade.

This is not only of importance to the interpretation of the location's individual features, but it also affects the chronological integrity or coherence of the site itself. Despite appearing to be a logical whole, consisting of a number of contemporaneous features (one hall replacing another, both encircled by a palisade), it seems that at least the greater hall may be Early Neolithic and the palisade may be a later Neolithic structure (or it may even be post-Neolithic). The lithics do not carry any information regarding the date of the smaller hall or the relationship between the two halls.

The composition of the Early and Late Neolithic sub-assemblages indicates that one is almost certainly ritual in character, whereas the status of the other is uncertain. No 'ordinary' finds were made from the Early Neolithic hall, and all finds were recovered from roof-bearing or wall postholes, rather than being scattered across the feature. One find is a well-executed, burnt leaf-shaped arrowhead in flint (apparently unused), and the assemblage also includes one unusually large bipolar core in pitchstone, two pitchstone blades, and four refitting fragments of a very large, heavily burnt, tabular piece of raw pitchstone. Experiments (Fischer *et al.* 1979, 22-7) have shown that, if lithics are covered by even small amounts of soil or ashes, they are minimally affected by for example house fires, and it is highly unlikely that the burnt flint arrowhead and the heavily burnt (and disintegrated) piece of raw pitchstone (deposited in postholes) were fire-crazed in connection with the destruction of the house. Moreover, the heavily burnt status of the raw pitchstone piece is reminiscent of the situation at Torrs Warren, where numerous pieces of burnt raw pitchstone were associated with large numbers of burnt scrapers in imported Antrim flint (cf., Cowie 1996, 60; Ballin 2009, 11). The latter situation may have been a case of ritual destruction of wealth (cf. Larsson 2004).

The composition of the finds from the palisade area is comparable to the composition of Late Neolithic domestic assemblages, although the finds seem to include higher proportions of scale-flaked/plano-convex knives, as well as other less common tool forms, than those of domestic assemblages. Many pieces are used, damaged or repaired/recycled; and it appears that attempts were made to exhaust the (exotic) raw material completely. The Late Neolithic assemblage is predominantly in flint (13 pieces), supplemented by one piece in chert, one in chalcedony and one in quartz. A small number of yellow/orange and cream flints are thought to represent local Scottish raw material, but most of the flint artefacts are either in marbled/dotted grey or (rarer) homogeneous dark-brown colours, suggesting importation from Yorkshire.

The Late Neolithic finds embrace nine tools, namely two scale-flaked knives, one plano-convex knife, one backed knife, one short end-scraper and four pieces with edge-retouch. The high tool ratio (56%) may largely be a result of the collection's residual character, recovery policies (ie, the lack of consistent sieving) and selective collection.

Due to the character of the site's unstratified finds, it is thought that the majority of these may also date to the Late Neolithic period: 1) 38 of 68 artefacts (56%) are in grey or (rarer) dark-brown Yorkshire flint; 2) the unmodified and modified flint tool blanks include four robust blades (due to fragmentation, it was not possible to determine the applied percussion technique); and 3) the tools include typical Late Neolithic tool forms, such as two scale-flaked knives, one combination tool (a scraper/scale-flaked knife), and one strike-a-light. Four pitchstone artefacts (one of which is a microblade) almost certainly date to the Early Neolithic period.

As the Late Neolithic finds are chronologically 'sandwiched' between earlier (the timber hall) and later (the cremation cemetery) ritual activities at the summit of Doon Hill, it is quite possible that this location is characterized by a continuum of ritual behaviour dating to the period Early Neolithic-Bronze Age (-Iron Age, if the smaller hall is dated to this period), and that the Late Neolithic assemblage was deposited in connection with ritual activities. However, it is not possible on the basis of the lithic collection itself, its composition and context, to safely determine whether the Late Neolithic finds from the palisaded area represent a settlement linked to ritual activities, an actual ritual site, or possibly a high status domestic hill-top settlement.

The three assemblages from Barnhouse, Ness of Brodgar, and Doon Hill are all combined flake-and-blade assemblages, based on hard percussion and the application of the Levallois-like technique (defined by finely facetted platform remnants).

For a summary of the category, see Chapter 3.3.

3.2.4 Assemblages from ritual sites

As the main purpose of Chapter 3 is, by defining assemblages from different site types, to characterize the assemblages of Airhouse and Overhowden in terms of the activities they represent, and as these assemblages were recovered from the vicinity of the Overhowden Henge, the most important elements of Chapter 3.2.4 are lithic collections from henges. Finds from stone circles (some of which are associated with henges), standing stones, pit clusters, and rock art sites are dealt with in a cursory

fashion. It should be emphasized that this chapter is not concerned with the structural details of the monuments, or the development of the monuments over time, only with their Late Neolithic lithic assemblages.

Henges

The archetypal, or classic, henge (Harding 1987, 30; Harding 2003) is a roughly circular or oval monument formed by an external bank and an inner ditch, and it has from one to four entrances. If there are more than one entrance, these tend to be opposed. The henge may (and may not) be associated with a wide variety of internal, as well as external, features (Clare 1986, 285), amongst which stone circles are probably the most iconic. One of the most relevant formal differences between types of henges, in terms of their flint assemblages, is arguably size, where the traditional henge belongs to an intermediate class, but there are also classes of more extreme henges, such as very small 'hengiform' monuments ('mini-henges'; Harding 2003, 29), as well as very large henges ('giant henges', Harding 1987, 31; 'henge enclosures', Harding 2003, 11). Henge monuments are generally dated to the Grooved Ware period. As the number of British henges is substantial, this section discusses lithics and henges in general terms, supported by various representative cases. A number of Scottish examples have been selected especially.

The relationship between henges and lithic assemblages is very precisely summed up by Holgate (1988, 50) who, in his volume on the 'Neolithic Settlement of the Thames Valley' writes: '*Henge monuments have also produced flint assemblages which vary in the range of implements they contain. Excavations at East Anglian and Upper Thames valley henges did not produce any implements, whilst most of the large Wessex henges produced a variety of implements*'. This is also noticed by Megaw and Simpson (1979, 155), who emphasizes the unusual character of the large artefact assemblage of Durrington Walls, underlining that '*... this feature is not on the whole characteristic of henges*'. It should also be noted that, when Clare (1986, 299) lists finds 'tipped into' the henge ditches soon after digging, the list embraces '*... charcoal, 'black material', 'domestic refuse' including pottery, and skeletal remains ...*', but it does not specifically mention flint artefacts.

At some mini-henges or classic henges, small lithic assemblages have been recovered from rare burial or votive contexts. At Corporation Farm (Oxfordshire), for instance, burnt fragments of a polished flint axehead were discovered in the interior (Harding 1987, 238), and at Dorchester IV (also Oxfordshire) a PTD was recovered from one of the cremations (ibid., 244). However, in many cases it is difficult to determine whether these finds actually pre- or post-date the monuments. At Arbor Low in Derbyshire, for example, a lithic assemblage from 'early ditch fills' includes one Early Neolithic leaf-shaped arrowhead as well as one Early Bronze Age barbed-and-tanged point (ibid., 110). As a general rule, substantial lithic assemblages appear only to be a feature of the larger 'giant' henges or 'henge enclosures'. Woodhenge (Wainwright 1979, 162), near Durrington Walls, yielded *c.* 250 flints and forms an exception from this rule. Most of the flints are from old land surfaces and from the monument's ditch. The bulk of this assemblage is flake and core waste, supplemented by some tools (predominantly scrapers, as well as two PTDs of Classes G and H).

Two giant henges have been excavated thoroughly and their substantial lithic assemblages presented in detail, namely those of Durrington Walls in Wiltshire and Mount Pleasant in Dorset (Wainwright & Longworth 1971; Wainwright 1979). Durrington Walls was the first giant henge to be excavated and published. The collection includes almost 12,000 flint artefacts from old land surfaces, from the Northern and Southern Circle, the Ditch, the Midden, as well as from Structures A and B. Flakes (≈ debitage) amount to 11,082 pieces (96.6%), cores 57 pieces (0.4%) and implements 333 pieces (3%). Slightly more than 3,000 pieces (26%) were retrieved from old land surfaces, with the bulk of the remainder deriving from the Southern Circle (59%). Apparently, the assemblages from the old land surface includes more debitage/fewer tools) than the other contexts (tool ratio *c.* 1%) but, as explained by Wainwright & Longworth (1971, 161) in connection with their Table X, the figures from the various contexts (debitage, cores, implements) are not directly comparable, as in some cases all lithics had been collected and in others only implements. The excavators interpreted some of the concentrations from the old land surface as knapping floors (ibid., 161).

It is not possible, on the basis of the published text, to determine with any degree of certainty whether finely faceted blanks and Levallois-like cores form parts of the finds, and the illustrations include almost no cores, just as they do not display the technological attributes of the blanks' bulbar ends. However, it is mentioned in passing (ibid., 168), that approximately 30% of the scrapers '... *possess faceted striking platforms which suggest pre-treatment of the cores*'. Wainwright & Longworth (ibid., 158) comment that '*The tendency in later Neolithic times for flakes to assume the broad squat outline is noticeable*', probably due to the switch at the Early/Late Neolithic transition from soft to hard percussion, but their measurements of blank length:width ratios (eg, ibid., 160) also show that substantial numbers of blades were still being produced.

The Late Neolithic tools (ibid., 164) are heavily dominated by scrapers (62%) and PTDs (17%), followed by retouched flakes (5%), knives (3%), piercers (2%), strike-a-lights (fabricators) (1.5%), and denticulates (1.5%). All other tool categories amount to 1% or less. They include, among other categories, five axeheads. A total of 59% of the tools were recorded from the Southern Circle, 14% from the Ditch, 10% from the old land surface and 4% from the Midden. The distribution of the various tool forms differ somewhat: Where 50% of the scrapers were retrieved from the Southern Circle and 24% from the surface of its platform, 81% of the PTDs were retrieved from the Southern Circle and 42% from the surface of its platform (ibid., 169; 171). A substantial number of finds were made in postholes, but it is almost impossible to determine which of these artefacts (if any) represent deliberate deposits, and which simply entered the postholes with the backfill.

The report does not mention any discoidal knives, polished-edge knives, polished-edge implements, or combined tools. These forms are so morphologically distinct that, even allowing for typological classification principles changing over time, it must be assumed that the assemblage does not include these forms. A fragmented curved sickle blade (ibid., 174) is most likely to be of a Bronze Age date (Clark 1934a) and, along with two barbed-and-tanged arrowheads, it probably post-dates the bulk of the assemblage. The PTDs almost exclusively belong to Clark's Classes G and H, and the knives are mostly scale-flaked and plano-convex forms.

The find circumstances (above) indicate that a significant proportion of the finds derive from obvious pre-monument contexts (old land surfaces), and it is quite likely that a considerable proportion of the remainder also predate the construction of the monument. However, it is also thought that proportions of the lithic material was deposited in connection with rituals at Durrington Walls, particularly in connection with the Southern Circle and on the platform.

Recent excavations at Durrington Walls (Chan 2009; forthcoming) focused partly on the same areas as those examined by Wainwright & Longworth (1971), but they also, and primarily, dealt with the East Entrance, from which more than 90% of the worked flints derive. Seven houses were discovered, flanking an avenue connecting the Southern Circle to the River Avon via the eastern entrance of the monument. The excavators found that the construction of the Durrington Walls bank post-dated most of the activities near the East Entrance, including the houses and middens.

The finds from the new excavations at the East Entrance are predominantly debitage and cores (98%). Like in the case of the old Durrington Walls assemblage, retouched flakes, scrapers and arrowheads are the most numerous implement categories, with other categories being knives, piercers, denticulates and notches. Chan (ibid.) notes that there is '... *a special relationship between the henge and oblique arrowheads*', and he suggests that the arrowheads were used for killing pigs for feasting, which were later butchered by the use of the site's knives and retouched flakes. As the finds from the East Entrance apparently predate the monument's bank, it is possible that this feasting represents ritual behaviour during, or before, the construction of the henge.

	Totals	Debi-tage	Cores	Tools	Scrapers	PTDs	Axe-heads	Serrated pieces	Inv. ret. knives	Strike-a-lights	Piercers	Ret. blades
Pre-enclosure settlement	1,164	1,128	7	29	15	3	2	6	2			1
Site IV, Ph 1	911	893	8	10	10							
Site IV, Ph 2, ditch segments	2,637	2,531	6	100	89	2		3	4			2
Site IV, later silts	1,594	1,510	4	80	64	1		1	10	1	1	2
Enclosure ditch	9,790	9,475	105	210	161	10	6	7	15	2	6	3
Palisade trench	5,730	5,506	56	168	131	8	4	12	7	3	2	1
TOTAL	**21,826**	**21,043**	**186**	**597**	**470**	**24**	**12**	**29**	**38**	**6**	**9**	**9**

Table 15. The Late Neolithic assemblage from Mount Pleasant – the most important contexts and the most important artefact categories. Based on Wainwright 1979, Tables VIII, IX, XI, XII, and XV, as well as parts of the volume's text.

In many respects, the published flint assemblage from Mount Pleasant (Wainwright 1979) is similar to the one from Durrington Walls (Wainwright & Longworth 1971). Due to the way the former material was presented, it is almost impossible to determine to which degree the Mount Pleasant knappers relied on the Levallois-like technique, and it is uncertain how large a proportion of the tools are simple edge-retouched pieces; the retouched blades in Table 15 clearly represent a selection of the most accomplished edge-retouched pieces. This table presents the most important trends in terms of the general composition of the Mount Pleasant material. Various diagrams, such as Wainwright (1979, Fig. 62), indicate that stout blades were still being produced (probably in the order of *c.* 20% of the debitage). As in the case of the Durrington Walls report, this report does not mention any polished-edge implements, discoidal knives, or combined tools. It is uncertain whether this is a true reflection of the assemblage.

In terms of more specific details, the Mount Pleasant assemblage differs somewhat from that of Durrington Walls. The former collection includes considerably fewer PTDs (4% against 17%) and more knives (6% against 3%) and serrated pieces (5% against less than 1%) than the latter. The two assemblages include approximately equal proportions of scrapers, axeheads, and strike-a-lights. As at Durrington Walls, it is thought that a proportion of the lithic finds represent pre-monument activity, and that other finds were deposited in connection with on-site rituals. Most of these rituals appear to have taken place around Site IV (the timber structure), the enclosure ditch, and the palisade trench. The different compositions of the two giant henge assemblages (in particular the much lower number of PTDs at Mount Pleasant), suggests that these rituals may have taken different forms at the two locations.

The account of the Late Neolithic sub-assemblage from Windmill Hill (Smith 1965, 104) presents an unusual assemblage, and the collection's composition suggests that it may have been deposited in connection with rituals performed in the areas around the Early Neolithic causewayed enclosure's ditches. It is possible that the

monument may simply have been taken over by Late Neolithic people as a form of 'pre-fabricated' giant henge (although the composition of the PTDs indicates a general date before the construction of most henges).

It is uncertain exactly how many of the site's flints date to the Late Neolithic, but Smith defines the following pieces as certainly or probably deriving from that period: 41 PTDs (18 chisel-shaped arrowheads, eight of the deviating group, five oblique arrowheads, one with polish, and nine unclassifiable fragments), six intact or fragmented polished/unpolished axeheads/chisels, 24 knives, one polished-edge knife, one polished-edge implement (scraper), 31 piercers, 26 strike-a-lights, and four serrated pieces or saws. The high number of PTDs, uncannibalized axeheads, knives and strike-a-lights, as well as the presence of various polished-edge pieces, clearly indicates that this assemblage is not the remains of an ordinary domestic settlement.

In the same volume, Smith (ibid., 224) gives an account of Late Neolithic finds from the giant henge at Avebury, as well as of finds made along the West Kennet Avenue, west of Avebury. In general, few artefacts were retrieved from the various contexts of the actual henge. Some of the finds appear to be pre-monument occupation debris (below the bank and from old land surfaces), whereas others are more obviously ritual deposits (from stone holes and the ditch). The former sub-assemblage includes typical domestic waste, such as many flakes and cores, and few tools, whereas for example the finds from the stone holes include one robust blade-scraper, one scale-flaked knife, one fabricator, one piercer, and one bifacial implement.

The so-called 'occupation site' along the West Kennet Avenue (ibid., 236) has been included in the present site category, as it forms part of the greater Avebury complex. Its assemblage includes the following main elements: 1,280 pieces of debitage (61% of which is burnt), 43 intact or shattered cores, and *c.* 1,051 tools (adding up to *c.* 2,374 pieces). The tools include a number of earlier (one microlith, one burin, and one leaf-shaped arrowhead) and later (seven barbed-and-tanged arrowheads) forms, but most are datable to the Late Neolithic period. A total of 516 pieces (or 49% of the tools) are scrapers; 95 pieces are PTDs (including 'triangular' pieces; ibid., Fig. 83.260) (or 9%); four are discoidal knives; four are polished-edge knives; one is a polished-edge implement (scraper); 35 are knives, most of which are scale-flaked specimens; *c.* 22 are strike-a-lights; 15+ are axeheads or fragments thereof; 85 are serrated pieces or saws (or 8%); and piercers amount to 73 pieces (or 7%). Thirty-six 'discoid object' represent a slightly confusing group – most likely many of these are unpolished discoidal knives or preforms of such implements (ibid., Fig.81.210), whereas others are clearly Levallois-like cores or fragments thereof (ibid., Fig. 81.209). Other categories account for up to 10 pieces each. The classifiable PTDs include 69 chisel-shaped arrowheads, eight pieces from the deviating group, and four oblique arrowheads.

Like the Late Neolithic finds from Windmill Hill, the assemblage from West Kennet Avenue definitely appear to be something other than simply a domestic site. Elements, which point in this direction, are the many PTDs, knives, strike-a-lights, and uncannibalized axeheads, as well as the presence of discoidal knives, polished-edge knives, and polished-edge implements. If the 'discoidal objects' actually include as many unpolished or roughed-out discoidal knives as the report indicates, this defines the assemblage as unusual indeed. At present, it is not possible to define the specific role of this site in the lives of Late Neolithic people, but it probably had a function related to the rituals taking place in this general area (as suggested by Smith; ibid., 212). This proposition is supported by the fact that many of the finds were made in pits or 'holes' (basically, small pits) along the avenue.

In summary, assemblages from Late Neolithic giant henges (and their satellite monuments) are characterized by the following elements:

- They generally include relatively large amounts of production waste (flakes and cores), although cores appear to be slightly less common than one would expect from comparison with traditional production or domestic sites (ie, they seem to have a skewed flake:core ratio);
- Scrapers and PTDs usually dominate the assemblages, or they make up substantial proportions of the implement total;
- Most of these assemblages usually include so-called 'fancy', prestige or specialized types, such as scale-flaked and plano-convex knives, fabricators and uncannibalized axeheads – due to the age of most of the giant henge excavations/publications, it is uncertain whether discoidal knives, polished-edge knives, and polished-edge implements are actually absent from the Durrington Walls and Mount Pleasant assemblages, but these forms are definitely present in the collections from Windmill Hill and West Kennet Avenue.

A study of the publications of the most significant Scottish henges and their lithic assemblages confirmed the general trends suggested above, that is, that classic British henges usually yield very small lithic assemblages, if any. No giant henges are known from Scotland. Below, a number of Scottish henge assemblages are discussed.

From the henge of Cairnpapple, West Lothian (Piggott 1950; Barclay 1999), a small number of flint flakes, two axehead fragments (Group VI, from Great Langdale in Cumbria, and Group VII, from Graig Lwyd in Wales), and one scraper were recovered. These finds represent material pre- or post-dating the henge monument. The author has been shown pitchstone artefacts (probably dating to the Early Neolithic period) collected in the vicinity of the henge (Ballin 2009), and the retrieval of obvious Early Neolithic exotic material from the general henge area (Arran pitchstone, as well as Cumbrian and Welsh axehead fragments), as well as the presence of Bronze Age burials, suggest that Cairnpapple was a site of significance before, during and after the 'active life' of the henge – although lithics formed no significant part of the rituals.

The henge at Knappers, Dunbartonshire (Davidson 1935; MacKay 1948; Ritchie & Adamson 1981) represents a similar continuum of activities, including a Late Neolithic henge and several Early Neolithic, Late Neolithic, and Early Bronze Age burials. Some finds were recovered from the surface (possibly representing a knapping floor), whereas a substantial number of lithic artefacts were retrieved from various burials, mostly cists. Some lithic finds are thought to be missing, but 57 pieces were examined by Wickham-Jones (1981a, 193) and an edge-polished flint axehead of Duggleby Type by Kenworthy (1981, 189). The latter was recovered from a cist, unfortunately unaccompanied by pottery.

The worked lithics are mainly in flint, but also include a handful of pieces in quartz and siltstone/mudstone. The fact that the majority of the flint objects are in grey or pale grey colours suggests that these pieces may have been procured from sources in the general Yorkshire area. The assemblage includes some stout blades (eg, a possible strike-a-light; Wickham-Jones 1981a, Fig. 7.2), and the assemblage appears generally to have been detached by the application of hard percussion. Wickham-Jones (ibid., 194) noted the presence of faceted platform remnants, probably indicating the application of the Levallois-like technique. In addition to the possible strike-a-light and the flint axehead, the assemblage includes two further secondarily modified pieces, namely a scale-flaked knife and a fragment of a ?mudstone axehead.

In summary, and considering the fact that a large proportion of the lithics derive from various cist burials (several of which might not date to the Late Neolithic period), the Knappers henge in itself yielded very low numbers of lithic artefacts.

The Balfarg/Balbirnie ceremonial complex in Fife (Mercer 1981; Mercer *et al.* 1988; Barclay & Russell-White 1993) includes a large variety of individual monuments, such as a henge, timber structures, pits and an enclosure dating to the Late Neolithic period; a Late Neolithic/Early Bronze Age ring-ditch and a more or less contemporary ring cairn; and a series of pits pre-dating the Late Neolithic period. The henge yielded an assemblage of 92 lithic artefacts, most of which are in flint. The colour scheme of the flints indicates that some were procured from local beaches, whereas a substantial number of pale grey pieces may be Yorkshire flint. Flakes were detached by soft as well as hard percussion. Wickham-Jones (1981b) notes that some flakes display platform faceting, which may indicate that those were manufactured by the application of the Levallois-like technique. It is not immediately clear from the report whether blades are present. Most of the collection is debitage, supplemented by one core and 10 implements, or fragments thereof. The implements include one backed microblade, two flakes struck from cannibalized polished flint axeheads, one PTD, one barbed-and-tanged arrowhead, one scraper, one scale-flaked knife, and several edge-retouched pieces.

Although most of the artefacts are thought to be Late Neolithic (as suggested by the use of hard percussion, the application of Levallois-like technique, Yorkshire flint, and the PTD), earlier (soft percussion, backed microblade) and later (the barbed-and-tanged arrowhead) material is also present. Wickham-Jones (ibid., 121) suggests that, as most of the lithic assemblage was recovered from an old ground surface pre-dating the henge, or from contexts such as postholes relating to the henge (possibly entering the postholes with the backfill), most of this collection is probably residual pre-Late Neolithic material (or at least pre-dating the construction of the henge).

This small unspectacular Late Neolithic assemblage may be the remains of a domestic site, which left no other indications of its character, or it may be the '...*debris of the builders*' (ibid., 120). Some flints were associated with an inhumation burial (cist) and a cremation, and the burial forms (cist and cremation), as well as the association in one case of the flints with a Beaker, suggest that they date to the Early Bronze Age.

A total of 256 lithic artefacts were recovered from the remainder of the Balfarg/Balbirnie complex (Wickham-Jones & Reed 1993), most of which are in flint, with the remainder including, *inter alia*, pitchstone. The largest sub-assemblage derives from the upper layers of the enclosure ditch, where they were associated with Beaker sherds. The bulk of the assemblage is debitage, supplemented by two cores, and a relatively large number of tools. The retouched pieces include forms such as scrapers, arrowheads (two leaf-shaped pieces and a barbed-and-tanged arrowhead), scale-flaked knives, finely serrated pieces (some with sickle gloss), and simple edge-retouched pieces. Two flakes were struck from a polished axehead.

Although some of the artefacts clearly pre-date the Late Neolithic period (leaf-shaped points, dominance of soft percussion, as well as 20 pieces of worked pitchstone; Ballin 2009) or post-date (one barbed-and-tanged point, thumbnail-scrapers, and association with Beakers in the ditch), a substantial minority of the finds may date to the Late Neolithic period. This is suggested by the fact that 16 of the site's flakes have finely faceted platform remnants, indicative of the Levallois-like technique. Although it is impossible to estimate the size of the Late Neolithic sub-assemblage precisely, due to the site's palimpsest character, it may be in the order of between one-quarter and one-third of the total lithic assemblage (50-75 pieces?).

Although a small number of lithic artefacts may have been deposited deliberately at the various monuments, the character of the assemblage is as unspectacular as that of the Balfarg henge, and it is probably reasonable to assume that most of the Late Neolithic finds are residual pieces, pre-dating the construction of the various monuments.

A total of 74 lithic artefacts were recovered from the North Mains henge in Perthshire (Wickham-Jones 1983), most of which are in flint, with the remainder including, *inter alia*, 10 pieces of pitchstone. More than half of the artefacts are from topsoil or surface collection, within as well as outwith the henge; seven pieces were recovered below or within the bank as well as in the ditch fill; and the remainder were found in Bronze Age contexts, such as burials.

Most of the assemblage is debitage, supplemented by one core and eight tools. The implements include two barbed-and-tanged arrowheads (both from burials), two scrapers (one of which is discoidal), and a scale-flaked knife. The vast majority of the assemblage clearly dates to either the Early Neolithic or Bronze Age periods. The former is suggested by the preference for medium- to soft hammers, as well as the presence of pitchstone (Ballin 2009), and the latter by the discoidal scraper, the arrowheads, and the burial contexts (associated with Beakers, Food Vessels, and Urns). Small amounts of Late Neolithic material is present, as suggested by flakes with finely faceted platform remnants, but the find contexts (above) indicate that these pieces are not associated with the henge.

Stone circles

As mentioned above, some henges are associated with stone circles It has been chosen to deal with monuments like Stonehenge, Stones of Stenness, and Ring of Brodgar in the present section, as those three impressive monuments are primarily visible in the landscape due to their massive megaliths.

Stonehenge in Wiltshire yielded little worked flint altogether: possible Grooved Ware, bone pins and flint strike-a-lights (fabricators) have been recovered from the site's so-called Aubrey holes (Harding 1987, 300). From excavations at Stones of Stenness in Orkney, nine lithic artefacts were recorded (eight flints and one piece of chert). Most of these are simple chips and flakes, but two pieces are plano-convex knives, or fragments thereof (Ritchie 1976, 25; Harding 1987, 389). One fragment of a plano-convex knife was associated with the site's central feature of four massive stones, whereas the rest came from topsoil and the ditch. Excavations at the Ring of Brodgar, also Orkney, yielded no lithic artefacts (Harding 1987, 388).

The small stone circle at Croft Moraig, Perthshire, was excavated by Piggott & Simpson (1971) in 1965. They conclude that this monument may be a small henge comparable to the Class II henge at Loanhead of Daviot in Aberdeenshire. The assemblage from the site includes a mixture of Neolithic and Bronze Age pottery, but no lithics. White quartz appears to have been scattered across the monument.

Calanais on Lewis, Western Isles, is a complex ritual monument, combining a stone circle, standing stones and a central cairn. Excavations at the site yielded 314 lithic artefacts, most of which is quartz supplemented by some flint and mylonite (Ballin forthcoming e). Most of the finds are thought to be residual settlement material predating the ritual monument, and the remainder of the finds are associated with the later cairn. Diagnostic lithic elements and analysis of the find contexts suggest that the bulk of the latter dates to the Early Bronze Age. Most likely, little or no lithic material was deposited at the ritual complex in the Late Neolithic period.

Like the henges discussed above, stone circles and stone circles-cum-henges appear in general not to be associated with lithic assemblages.

Standing stones

Few excavations have been carried out in connection with standing stones. One such excavation was undertaken at the site of Duntreath Standing Stones in Stirlingshire (MacKie 1972). The monument consists of five standing stones arranged in a straight line from the north-west towards the south-east on the highest part of a broad ridge. The archaeological investigation yielded a small lithic assemblage which included two pieces of pitchstone. It was not possible to find the assemblage in the museum stores, but a photograph of the finds, kindly provided by Dr MacKie, suggests that the pitchstone artefacts are proximal fragments of either blade-like flakes or blades of the sort most commonly associated with earlier Neolithic sites.

There had been a fire on the old ground surface, immediately beside the southernmost stone, which left traces of ash and charcoal, and the lithics were found in a context stratigraphically later than this layer. A charcoal sample from the old ground surface was subsequently dated rather broadly to 4500-2500 cal BC (GX-2781), which embraces the period Late Mesolithic to Late Neolithic. As the lithic assemblage from the old ground surface includes not only definitely pre Late Neolithic blade material in pitchstone, as well as the fragment of an Early Bronze Age barbed-and-tanged point, this context is undoubtedly disturbed.

However, the small number of finds (one or two of which may be Late Neolithic) supports the general impression from the discussion of henges and stone circles (above) that lithic assemblages were rarely deposited at ritual monuments during this period.

Rock art sites

Two Scottish rock art sites have been the focus of recent archaeological investigation. The site of Torbhlaren in Argyll & Bute was excavated by Dr Andrew Jones of the University of Southampton (Jones & O'Connor 2007) and the finds are presently being examined by Dr Lamdin-Whymark; the rock art of Ben Lawers in Perthshire is being investigated by Professor Richard Bradley from Reading University (Spicer 2007). Both sites yielded a small number of pitchstone artefacts and, in his discussion of Scottish pitchstone distribution, the present author suggested that these finds (which include narrow blades) may be residual Early Neolithic pieces. From both site's, a quantity of worked quartz was recovered, and it is presently being considered whether this material represents traditional quartz assemblages, or whether the quartz flakes and debris was formed in connection with the production of the actual rock art (Lamdin-Whymark forthcoming).

Pit clusters

Clusters of ceremonial pits are known from Early (eg, Cowie Road, Stirling; Rideout 1997) as well as Late Neolithic sites (eg, Midmill, Aberdeenshire; Ballin forthcoming h). In connection with archaeological investigations at Midmill SE, Kintore, Aberdeenshire, Murray Archaeological Services Ltd. discovered numerous archaeological features, some of which dated to prehistoric times and some to later periods. From the prehistoric features and their surroundings, 249 lithic artefacts were recovered. They were distributed across two main areas, Area 1 (64 pieces) and Area 2 (180 pieces) (Table 16)[2]. Although Area 1 was dominated by an Early Bronze Age cremation complex, associated with Beaker pottery, the lithics were mostly retrieved from pits containing Late Neolithic Grooved Ware (Pits 7, 28, and 29); Only 10 pieces were recovered from Early Bronze Age features (Contexts 46-8, 50-54). Area 2 was associated with considerable amounts of Late Neolithic Impressed Ware (pottery identification by Alison Sheridan, National Museums Scotland).

---

[2] A third area at Midmill was excavated after the production of the present volume. It only yielded 26 lithic artefacts, which are thought to represent an Early Bronze Age domestic site.

		Area 1					Area 2							
	Eval., unstrat.	Pit C7	Pit C28	Pit C29	Other contexts	Total, Area 1	Hearth C26	Buried soil C27	Posthole C64	Pit C65	Posthole C68	Other contexts	Total, Area 2	Grand total
Debitage														
Chips		2	2		1	5		1	2	21	2		26	*31*
Flakes	4	6	17	5	13	*41*	8	30	7	38	7	9	*99*	*144*
Blades		1	2	3	1	*7*	1	5		4	1	3	*14*	*21*
Microblades		1				*1*				1		1	*2*	*3*
Indeterminate pieces	1				2	*2*		1		5		2	*8*	*10*
Crested pieces							1	1					*2*	*2*
Total debitage	*5*	*10*	*21*	*8*	*17*	*56*	*10*	*38*	*9*	*69*	*10*	*15*	*151*	*211*
Cores														
Single-platform cores				1		*1*								*1*
Levallois-like cores								3		1			*3*	*4*
Irregular cores							1	1				1	*3*	*3*
Bipolar cores				1		*1*	1	3		5			*9*	*10*
Total cores				*2*		*2*	*2*	*7*		*6*		*1*	*16*	*18*
Tools														
?Microburins			1			*1*								*1*
Short end-scrapers								2				1	*3*	*3*
Scraper-edge fragments		1				*1*								*1*
Scale-flaked knives								1					*1*	*1*
Truncated pieces												1	*1*	*1*
Serrated pieces				1		*1*	1			2			*3*	*4*
Piercers							1					1	*2*	*2*
Notched pieces				1		*1*								*1*
Edge-retouched pieces		1			1	*2*		1				1	*2*	*4*
Stone axehead fragments										1			*1*	*1*
Total tools		2		1	3	*6*	2	4		3		4	*13*	*19*
TOTAL	**5**	**10**	**23**	**9**	**22**	**64**	**14**	**49**	**9**	**78**	**10**	**20**	**180**	**249**
Finely faceted pieces		2	1		3	6	1	7		5	2	1	16	22
Exotic pieces		3	16	2	1	22		1					1	23

Table 16. General artefact list. To give an overview of the distribution of all diagnostic elements, the distribution of pieces with finely faceted platform remnants (from Levallois-like cores) and pieces in exotic flint are shown below the actual artefact list.

The lithic assemblage is heavily dominated by flint (98%), supplemented by artefacts in sandstone, quartz, and quartzite, as well as one fragment of a polished axehead in Cumbrian tuff. The flint includes a number of subgroups, distinguished mainly by varying colours and fineness. A small proportion of the recovered artefacts are in the traditional reddish, fine-grained flint of eastern Scotland (Stevenson 1948, 181), but the assemblage also includes a small number of relatively crude flints which may have derived from the Buchan Ridge Gravels near Peterhead (Bridgeland *et al.* 1997; Saville 2006). However, most of the flint is represented by two subgroups, which are relatively similar in terms of visual attributes and flaking properties. One, the largest, group is thought to be local

flint from north-east Scotland, whereas the other is likely to have been imported, probably from Yorkshire in north-east England. Thirty flints are burnt.

The Area 1 sub-assemblage (the Grooved Ware assemblage) includes 64 pieces. Fifty-six of these are debitage, whereas two are cores, and six are tools. Among other things, the debitage embraces seven regular blades. All technologically definable blanks were manufactured by the application of hard percussion, with 9% having been detached from Levallois-like cores. Only two cores were recovered from this part of the excavation, namely one single-platform core and one bipolar core. The flatness of the former, in conjunction with its surviving

	Area 1	Area 2
Core ratio, Pits 7, 28, 29	0.0%	
Core ratio, Pit 65		7.7%
Tertiary pieces	80%	52%
Bipolar ratio, flakes and blades	0.0%	20%
Definitely exotic pieces	35%	0.5%
Burnt pieces	28%	6%

Table 17. Significant differences between the Late Neolithic assemblages from Areas 1 and 2.

broad platform, indicates that it may be the remains of a completely exhausted Levallois-like core. This area also yielded six tools, namely one dubious microburin, one scraper-edge fragment, one notched piece, one serrated piece, and two pieces with edge-retouch. The tool blanks are two flakes, two blades, one microblade and one abandoned core – all technologically definable pieces were detached by hard percussion.

The Area 2 sub-assemblage (the Impressed Ware assemblage) includes 180 pieces. A total of 151 are debitage, whereas 16 are cores, and 13 are tools. The debitage from this area embraces, *inter alia*, 14 blades and two crested pieces. It was possible to identify the percussion technique applied to detach 92 flakes and blades, with 80% having been manufactured by the use of hard percussion and 20% in bipolar technique; 9% of all flakes and blades were detached from Levallois-like cores. The 16 cores include three main categories, namely Levallois-like (four pieces), irregular (three pieces), and bipolar (nine pieces) specimens. The 13 implements from Area 2 include three short end-scrapers, one scale-flaked knife, one truncated piece, three serrated pieces, two piercers, two pieces with edge-retouch and one fragment of a polished axehead. The flint tool blanks are seven flakes, three blades, one microblade and one thermal flake – apart from one bipolar microblade, all technologically definable tool blanks were detached by hard percussion.

Apart from approximately a handful of pieces from late features relating to the Early Bronze Age cremation complex, the two sub-assemblages from Areas 1 and 2 appear homogeneous and probably date to the Late Neolithic period. Both sub-assemblages include few diagnostic types, but scale-flaked knives and serrated pieces are commonly found in Late Neolithic contexts (above). As it is difficult to distinguish between the darker local flints and the grey Yorkshire flints, only the dark-brown flints were recorded as certainly exotic, although it is thought that many of the grey pieces from Area 2 also represent importation. The most diagnostic feature of both sub-assemblages is the application of the Levallois-like technique. The association with different pottery styles indicates that one Late Neolithic assemblage (Area 1: Grooved Ware pottery) may be slightly later than the other (Area 2: Impressed Ware pottery).

Apart from one core from the topsoil and one from the early Bronze Age cremation complex (CAT 73), there were no cores in Area 1, whereas 8.9% of the Area 2 assemblage (7.7% of Pit 65) is made up of Levallois-like, irregular and bipolar cores (Table 17). This indicates that the blanks found in Area 1 may have been produced elsewhere, whereas the many cores recovered from Area 2 indicate on-site reduction. The fact that the finds from Area 1 include no bipolar blanks, whereas 20% of the (almost contemporary) blanks from Area 2 were produced by the application of hammer and anvil, suggests that the blanks from Area 1 represent a selection of better flakes and blades from the first stages of an operational schema, whereas the blanks from Area 2 represent material from all stages of an operational schema, including products from the final exhaustion of abandoned platform-cores by bipolar technique. The possibility of the Area 1 assemblage representing selection is further supported by 1) a much higher ratio of tertiary pieces (80% against Area 2's 52%), and 2) a much higher ratio of clearly exotic flints (35% against Area 2's 0.5%).

The fact that almost 20% of the Late Neolithic Area 1 assemblage is affected by exposure to fire, against 6% of the Area 2 assemblage, suggests that the Late Neolithic finds from Area 1 may represent ritual activities, possibly including some form of destruction of artefacts by fire (cf. Larsson 2004), whereas the lithic assemblage from Area 2 may be the product of mainly domestic activities. This interpretation is supported by the character of the main Late Neolithic features, as listed in Table 17: Where the features of Area 1 are dominated by three pits (Contexts 7, 28, and 29), those of Area 2 are dominated by a hearth (Context 26), buried soil (Context 27), two possible postholes (Contexts 64, and 68), and a pit (Context 65). The fact that Pit 65 includes 7.7% cores, against none in the Area 1 pits, implies that the former may simply be a domestic rubbish pit, whereas the contents of Pits 7, 28, and 29 may have been selected especially for the occasion. Neither assemblage includes any 'fancy' artefact forms, with a flake-based scale-flaked knife and mostly blade-based serrated pieces being the most accomplished implements recovered.

During a recent excavation by Glasgow University's Archaeological Research Division (GUARD) at Laigh Newton, East Ayrshire (Ballin forthcoming i), a small assemblage was recovered from the site's central part (22

Fig. 33. Sub-triangular polished knife (Evans 1897, Fig. 256). According to Clark's typology (Clark 1932b, 41), this piece corresponds to a discoidal knife of Type II.

pieces). The central sector of the project area included a number of prehistoric features, such as a cluster of pits; a small rectilinear, gully-formed feature thought to be a building; and several stray pits. A mixed pottery assemblage, including Impressed Ware and Grooved Ware, was retrieved from this sector (Beverley Ballin Smith pers. comm.). It is possible that this pit-associated assemblage represents ritual behaviour, like that of Midmill Area 1. Although several of the site's sectors include likely Late Neolithic artefacts, typo-technological composition and raw material preferences indicate that only the central sector is likely to be dominated by Late Neolithic material.

This assemblage is mainly in flint (supplemented by, *inter alia*, one piece of pitchstone), and *c.* one-third of the flint is thought to be Yorkshire flint. It also includes one blade and several pieces identifiable as blanks from Levallois-like cores. One of four tools is a sophisticated, sub-triangular form of discoidal flint knife, with three slightly convex, acute edges. Its dorsal face was formed entirely by invasive retouch, whereas the ventral face displays invasive retouch along two of the three edges. In terms of outline, it corresponds to a polished discoidal knife from Kempston, near Bedford, England (Fig. 33). Another tool is a flake from a polished flint implement (probably an axehead), with the remainder being simple edge-retouched pieces.

Assemblages from Late Neolithic ritual sites are summarized in Chapter 3.3.

3.2.5 Assemblages from burials

In Scotland, Late Neolithic burial goods are mostly known from secondary burials in communal Early Neolithic monuments (although see Kenworthy 1977; Ritchie & Adamson 1981; Kenworthy 1981), whereas in England (particularly Derbyshire and Yorkshire) separate Late Neolithic burials occur. The latter are generally referred to as Early Individual Burials or burials of the Towthorpe Tradition. However, even in England, these Late Neolithic burials are not common. Green (1980, 110), for example,

talks of '*The virtual absence of burial as an attribute of the Rinyo-Clacton culture ...*'.

The principle of the Early Individual Burials is that individuals are buried in shafts, pits or cists, covered by barrows, usually accompanied by objects selected from a limited group of relatively sophisticated grave goods (Clarke *et al.* 1985, 63). Lithic objects include Seamer/Duggleby polished-edge axeheads/adzeheads, PTDs, discoidal and polished-edge knives, fabricators and, on occasion, simpler tool forms or flakes and blades. A burial from Liff's Lowe in Derbyshire included a kite-shaped arrowhead, defining this burial as later Early Neolithic and probably one of the earliest Early Individual Burials. Other potential objects in these graves are ceramic vessels, antler/stone maceheads, boar's tusk and beaver incisor implements, jet beads and sliders, and chalk cylinders. For an overview of the most spectacular of these burials, see Clarke *et al.* (1985, 246-251).

Late Neolithic artefacts are frequently recovered from Scottish chambered monuments, but the present chapter only presents a limited number of representative cases. Henshall's two tomes (1963, 1972) on Chambered Tombs in Scotland provide an excellent overview.

The chambered tomb of *Calf of Eday (Long)*, Orkney, contained much pottery, as well as several pieces of worked flint. Some of the flint implements are of Early Neolithic dates, but a polished edge-implement is likely to represent a Late Neolithic deposition.

From the tomb of *Unstan*, Orkney, a similarly impressive assemblage was recovered, including pottery, flint and stone. Again, most of the flints are likely to be Early Neolithic, but a fabricator (strike-a-light) on a robust blade and a fragmented polished-edge knife are typical Late Neolithic implements.

The *Camster Round* burial from Caithness, yielded some sherds of pottery and several interesting pieces of worked flint. The most impressive lithic object is a long, slender plano-convex knife with one polished cutting-edge. It corresponds accurately to several of the pieces illustrated by Manby (1974, Fig. 36-37) in his discussion of Yorkshire's more elegant polished-edge knives. The assemblage also includes two PTD arrowheads. The polished-edge knife and the two PTDs are all in grey (Yorkshire?) flint, and the fact that one scraper and one blade with bilateral retouch are also in grey flint suggests that those two pieces may also date to the Late Neolithic period.

From the chamber of the *Ormiegill* tomb, also Caithness, small amounts of pottery were recovered, with one stone macehead and a small group of flints. The latter included three relatively sophisticated chisel-shaped and oblique arrowheads, one end of a polished-edge knife, and a utilized flake of grey-buff flint. The three PTDs are in the dark-brown flint, which characterizes the later part of the British Late Neolithic period (Chapter 2.2). In addition to this small Late Neolithic group, the chamber contained a small Early Neolithic leaf-shaped point and a probably Early Bronze Age thumbnail-scraper, both in light-brown flint (Clarke *et al* 1985, Fig. 2.8).

The southern chamber of *Tulloch of Assery A*, Caithness, only contained a small flint assemblage. However, one implement is a chisel-shaped arrowhead (although more extensively modified than one would usually expect from these pieces), and clearly date to the Late Neolithic, and a grey blade and two flakes in grey flint may also date to this period.

The chambered cairn of *Nether Largie*, Kilmartin Valley, Argyll & Bute, yielded a sizeable collection of pottery and a small assemblage of flint artefacts. The latter embraces a knife fragment and part of a flake, both in grey (Yorkshire?) flint, as well as a flake in speckled buff flint with one edge retouched. The illustration of the latter (Henshall 1972, 302) shows that this piece has significant damage to its cutting-edge (impact damage?), and it may be an expedient chisel-shaped arrowhead.

From the chambered tomb of *Kilchoan*, Kilmartin Valley, Argyll & Bute, sherds of a Beaker were retrieved, as well as three scrapers in speckled grey (Yorkshire?) flint. One of the three scrapers may be based on a stout blade, and it has full, relatively acute retouch of both lateral sides. It may be a composite implement, combining the functions of a scraper and a scale-flaked knife.

In addition to a small number of sherds, the burial chamber at *Tormore 1*, Arran, contained a stone macehead and an interesting mainly Late Neolithic flint assemblage. The latter includes two plano-convex knives with one or two polished cutting-edges (Manby 1974, Fig. 36-37), as well as one scraper, eight retouched pieces and several unmodified blanks in either grey or dark-brown flint. One small blade and two flakes in pitchstone probably date to the Early Neolithic period.

As mentioned above, two possible Early Individual Burials are known from Scotland, namely those of *Greenbrae, Cruden*, Aberdeenshire (Kenworthy 1977) and *Knappers*, Dunbartonshire (Davidson's Find-Spot 1; Ritchie & Adamson 1981; Kenworthy 1981). The former burial was discovered around 1812, but the find circumstances are uncertain. Smith (1974, 41) describes the original account of the discovery as 'confused' (PSAS 22 1988, 366-7). This burial contained one Seamer/Duggleby polished-edge axe-/adzehead as well as amber and jet beads (Kenworthy 1977; Clarke *et al.* 1985, 250, Fig. 3.38). The latter burial was a boulder-built cist, with a large coverslab and a decorated end-stone (pecked concentric rings and a U-shaped motif), and it only contained a fine edge-polished adzehead of Duggleby Type.

It is quite possible that many more Neolithic grave monuments described by Henshall (1963; 1972) contained Late Neolithic artefacts, but the above pieces are the most obvious, and they provide an overview of a pattern. The burial goods seem to be dominated by artefacts in exotic Yorkshire flint, possibly because of the appearance of this raw material (visual qualities of the flint), but probably more likely due to the fact that artefacts in Yorkshire flint (which would have been collected in north-east England as fairly large nodules or cobbles) tended to be considerably larger and more impressive than artefacts based on smaller local flint pebbles.

Assemblages from Late Neolithic burial sites are summarized in Chapter 3.3.

3.3 Definition of assemblage types - summary

Below, the assemblages discussed in Chapter 3.2 are briefly summarized by site type.

Extraction sites

Extraction sites are generally characterized by much debris and restricted formal variation. Their assemblages are dominated by the following artefact categories: 1) If the site is based on quarrying rather than collection: extraction tools (eg, pics and points); 2) raw material stocks (raw nodules or shaped/decorticated core rough-outs); 3) waste from primary production; 4) cores (many of which are of Levallois-like form) and unmodified flake and blade blanks (for export out of the site); and 5) few or no tools (any tools would tend to be informal/expedient).

Domestic settlements

Lithic assemblages from domestic settlements are frequently numerically large, and often associated with equally large assemblages of Peterborough/Impressed Ware or Grooved Ware pottery. They tend to be defined by the following elements: 1) A relatively large number of different everyday (ie, non-fancy') tool forms; 2) domination by one, two or three formal implement categories, where scrapers are usually the most common tool type (up to half of all tools), with other important formal types being arrowheads (eg, Storey's Bar Road and East Lochside) and serrated pieces (eg, Honington); 3) apart from at Storey's Bar Road (with its particular economical basis linked to its status as a fen-site), informal tools (expedient edge-retouched pieces) are very common; 4) although discoidal knives, scale-flaked/plano-convex knives and strike-a-lights may be present (although not common), other 'fancy' tool types (polished axeheads, polished-edge knives, polished-edge implements and combined forms) tend to be absent; and 5) although polished axeheads are rare on domestic sites, detached flakes from recycled axeheads are not uncommon.

Settlements functionally linked to ritual sites

In general terms, assemblages from these settlements tend to be relatively numerically large, and they may be associated with unusual features or structures (at Barnhouse and Ness of Brodgar, considerably larger-than-average houses). They are generally characterized by the following attributes: 1) In Scotland, a higher proportion of exotic flint than experienced in connection with assemblages from ordinary domestic settlements in the same general area; 2) the same general typological variation as that of assemblages from common domestic sites (ie, a relatively large number of different everyday tool forms, with one, two or three formal implement categories dominating); 3) in contrast to assemblages from common domestic sites, they usually include higher proportions of fancy tool forms; and 4) caches are occasionally present at these sites.

Ritual sites

Most assemblages from ritual sites – including mini-henges and classic henges, stone circles, standing stones, and rock art sites – include no or very few lithic artefacts. If any lithics are present at these sites (and they can be dated to the time of the monuments), they may be tools, such as scale-flaked or plano-convex knives associated with the sites' central features (eg, Stones of Stenness), or other fancy objects associated with, for example, burials (eg, Dorchester IV).

The giant henges tend to have numerically large assemblages, which may have been deposited before the construction of the henges (by the builders?) or during the life-time of the monuments (sacrifices?). In both cases, it is thought that the assemblages, or parts thereof, may have been accumulated in connection with ritual feasting. These assemblages are characterized by: 1) Much production waste (flakes and cores); 2) greatly varied tool assemblages, which include some ordinary tool categories as well as many categories of rarer and so-called 'fancy' types; 3) scrapers and arrowheads tend to dominate, with formal knives, serrated pieces, strike-a-lights and uncannibalized axeheads being common or at least present; 4) arrowheads appear to be particularly

important (and in some cases they dominate); 5) due to the age (excavation and publication) of the assemblages from Durrington Walls and Mount Pleasant, it is uncertain whether the absence of discoidal knives, polished-edge knives, polished-edge implements and combined tools is real, or whether some may have been overlooked or classified according to different principles than the ones applied in connection with the present report – such pieces are present in the assemblages from West Kennet Avenue and Windmill Hill.

Late Neolithic ritual pit clusters may yield small lithic assemblages, which tend to be dominated by production waste, supplemented by unspectacular tool forms. However, at Laigh Newton, a fragmented discoidal knife was recovered. Assemblages from these sites may include above-average proportions of flint, possibly relating to the ritual destruction of wealth. Although no giant henges are known from Scotland, the assemblages from Midmill and Laigh Newton, as well as the slightly enigmatic assemblage from Doon Hill, indicate that Scottish assemblages from ritual monuments may generally include above-average proportions of exotic flint.

Burials

Lithic objects from Early Individual Burials (the Towthorpe Burial Tradition) generally include Seamer/ Duggleby polished-edge axeheads/adzeheads, PTDs, discoidal and polished-edge knives, fabricators and, on occasion, simpler tool forms or flakes and blades. Other potential objects in these graves are ceramic vessels, antler/stone maceheads, boar's tusk and beaver incisor implements, jet beads and sliders, and chalk cylinders. The deposited flint artefacts from Scottish Late Neolithic graves include Seamer/Duggleby polished-edge axes/adzes (Greenbrae and Knappers), PTDs, scale-flaked and plano-convex knives, polished-edge knives, polished-edge implements, fabricators, combined tools, well-executed flake- and blade-scrapers, and unmodified blanks.

3.4 Functional characterization of the Airhouse and Overhowden sites

Frequently, the character of a Late Neolithic site is revealed as much by the association with features and other find groups as by their lithic assemblages, but in the Airhouse/Overhowden case, only the lithic assemblage is available to the analyst. In terms of features, it is known that the two sites are situated in close proximity to a classic henge, the Overhowden henge. However, as the finds were recovered by surface collection, rather than by excavation, it is uncertain whether the prehistoric sites had any houses on them, or whether any houses were, for example, larger than normal Late Neolithic houses (as at Barnhouse and Ness of Brodgar). It is equally uncertain whether the sites were associated with, for example, palisades (eg, Doon Hill), pits (eg, Midmill) or burials (flat graves). Due to the three-dimensional character of some Scottish features, it is almost certain that the two sites – with their flat, megalith-free topography – were not associated with any quarries, stone circles, standing stones, rock art or monumental burials. In terms of defining the sites, it would have been helpful to know 1) if pottery had been deposited at the sites, 2) the types of pottery deposited, and 3) how this pottery had been deposited, but ceramic finds are entirely absent, possibly because it was not collected in the first place, or because it was not offered to National Museums Scotland by the finders.

As explained in Chapter 3.2, some site types are characterized by large volumes of debitage and some by the complete, or almost complete, absence of debitage, but, again, due to the find circumstances, and circumstances of purchase, it is not possible to say with any degree of certainty whether the two sites originally produced debitage or had debitage deposited at them. The fact that Airhouse and Overhowden represent two sites, and that both sites represent activities throughout the Late Neolithic period, with sporadic activity in the later part of the Early Neolithic and earlier part of the Early Bronze Age, makes it highly unlikely that no debitage was deposited at the locations at any time, and the lack of debitage *probably* represents a recovery bias, as well as post-collection selection.

In Chapter 3.1.1, it was attempted to estimate ('guesstimate') the original size of the combined Airhouse/Overhowden assemblage, and even admitting to the uncertainties of the calculations, it is possible to state that the original assemblage (as deposited in the past) must have been considerable. As practically all ritual sites (bar giant henges), as well as burials, are characterized by the recovery of small or no lithic assemblages, the probable numerical size of the combined assemblage in itself refers the two sites to a small group of possible site types. The lack of an obvious quarry, in conjunction with the fact that extraction sites are usually characterized by relatively few tools from a narrow tool spectrum, rules out the possibility that the Airhouse and Overhowden sites could belong to this site category (despite the usually high number of finds recovered from quarry sites and their surroundings). And, although the present assemblage has many similarities to assemblages from giant henges – not least in terms of the notable dominance of PTDs and the presence of many 'fancy' tool types – the absence of such a monument, and the fact that a classic henge is situated a few hundred metres from the two sites, rules out this option. This basically leaves the question as to whether the Airhouse and Overhowden sites should be defined as traditional domestic sites (whether economically broad-spectred or exploiting an economical niche) or whether they are 'settlements functionally linked to a ritual site' (in this case, the Overhowden Henge)?

Assemblages from both site types are characterized by including a relatively large variety of everyday tool types, with scrapers forming a substantial group. However, where PTDs (simpler and 'fancy' variants) only form

a numerically notable category on a small number of domestic sites (such as Storey's Bar Road, with its unique fenland economy), they generally form significant proportions of assemblages from giant henges, sites linked to henges, as well as burials. In terms of its high number of PTDs, the combined Airhouse/Overhowden assemblage defines Airhouse and Overhowden as most certainly *not* traditional domestic sites.

Although discoidal knives, scale-flaked/plano-convex knives, and strike-a-lights may be present at some domestic sites, they tend to be more common in non-domestic contexts, and uncannibalized polished axeheads/adzeheads, polished-edge knives, polished-edge implements and combined tools (such as, scale-flaked knives/scrapers) are almost completely absent from ordinary domestic sites. In terms of its proportions of 'fancy' and less common tool forms, the Airhouse/Overhowden assemblage must be defined as deriving from settlements with other functions than those of conventional domestic sites.

Another important element in connection with the characterization of the two sites is raw material preference. It is difficult to deal with this issue, as the presently available Late Neolithic assemblages from Scotland may not be representative in terms of the variation across the prehistoric totality, that is, that many of the presently available assemblages appear to represent other than conventional domestic sites. It is obvious that both assemblages are almost completely in Yorkshire flint (93%), as are most Scottish Late Neolithic sites from the Central Belt and southern Scotland, but as the majority of the well-known Late Neolithic locations from this area are unusual (ritual/high-status?) sites, it is impossible to determine whether this raw material preference reflects the two sites' status (and that of most other known Late Neolithic sites from southern Scotland) as 'unusual' or whether it merely reflects this area's relatively close proximity to the flint sources in north-east England.

The situation further to the north is somewhat clearer, and suggests that a high proportion of exotic flint may be related to a Late Neolithic site's status as 'unusual'. The fact that domestic Late Neolithic assemblages recovered in the Buchan Ridge area in Aberdeenshire are entirely in local gravel flint may merely reflect the fact that the parent sites were located right on top of a rich resource of this type of flint. However, the fact that the finds from domestic East Lochside in Angus only include 4% of exotic flint, whereas those from the ritual pits at Midmill in Aberdeenshire (further towards the north, and further away from the Yorkshire sources) include at least 35% suggests that non-domestic sites include higher proportions of exchanged (high-status?) material. This proposition is supported by the situation in Orkney, where sites near the island group's two massive stone circles-cum-henges yielded not only substantial numbers of artefacts in Yorkshire flint, but also surprisingly high numbers of artefacts in Arran pitchstone, whereas the domestic site of Pool on Sanday only yielded small amounts of exotic flint and no pitchstone.

In summary, it is possible to safely classify the sites of Airhouse and Overhowden as 'settlements functionally linked to a ritual site' (*in casu*, the Overhowden Henge). However, it should be borne in mind that 1) the site categories employed in this paper represent approximations to a prehistoric reality, and that, in prehistory, some sites could have been hybrid forms of the site categories defined in Chapter 3.2, and 2) occasionally, circumstances of discovery and recovery make it difficult to precisely define some sites. As shown in Chapter 3.2.3, the way the Doon Hill site in East Lothian was excavated and recorded makes it almost impossible to determine whether the Late Neolithic finds from the palisaded area represent a settlement linked to ritual activities, an actual ritual site, or possibly a high status domestic hill-top settlement. The same problem arrises when the analyst attempts to classify the West Kennet Avenue find concentration as to site type (Chapter 3.2.4). In the present paper, this site was dealt with in the chapter on ritual sites (henges), as the finds were most likely deposited in connection with activities linked to the Avenue from the Avebury giant henge, and thus to activities associated with the general Avebury ritual complex. However, without the Avebury connection, the site could just as well have been classified as a 'pit cluster'.

Another important point to make relates to the sites' exact dates. As indicated by the composition of the Airhouse/ Overhowden assemblage (Chapter 2.5), most of the finds were deposited during the Late Neolithic period, and it is likely that approximately half of those were deposited in the Impressed Ware period, and the other half in the Grooved Ware period (see for example the composition of the PTDs; Chapter 2.5.2). It is generally accepted (Harding 1987, 48; Harding 2003, 12) that most classic henges (if not all) were constructed in the Grooved Ware period, suggesting that, at Airhouse and Overhowden, the same activities took place before and after the construction of the henge. Or in other words: those two sites may have been special places linked to the activities at the henge in the Grooved Ware period, but they were equally special places in the Impressed Ware period.

In his preliminary paper on recent discoveries at Durrington Walls, Chan (2009) suggests that many of the numerous implements found at that site are related to ritual feasting (before, during, and after the construction of the monument?), and that the many PTDs may be related to the ritual? '... *shooting of pigs prior to their slaughtering for feasting*'. A similar scenario could be imagined for Airhouse and Overhowden, where ritual feasting took place at those sites – prior to, as well as after, the construction of Overhowden Henge. In the Durrington Walls case, the suggested interpretation is supported by the excavation of middens whereas, at the two sites in the Scottish Borders, no bone was recovered.

It is not uncommon to find that lithics deposited at Late Neolithic ritual sites or in Late Neolithic burials were new when deposited (eg, Stoneyhill Cairn 7/17 [Pit 7183]; Suddaby & Ballin forthcoming), but – almost without exception – the finds from Airhouse and Overhowden have clear macroscopic traces of wear (as have those recovered from Doon Hill): most PTDs are slightly fragmented, and the intact pieces have chipped cutting-edges (the chisel-shaped pieces) or tips (the oblique arrowheads and those of the deviating group); the scale-flaked and plano-convex knives generally have either chipped edges or macroscopically visible gloss from the cutting/sickling of grasses or cereals; most scrapers have overhanging edge areas from heavy-duty scraping; the strike-a-lights have clearly abraded terminals; and so forth. The scenario presented by this cursory use-wear analysis indicates that the activities taking place at the two sites were much more broad-spectred than simply killing and eating pigs, and it is possible that both sites were generally high-status settlements, such as the seats of powerful local Big Men (or, as suggested by other parts of Late Neolithic material culture: 'budding' chiefs in a developing prestige economy; Clarke *et al.* 1985), where traditional domestic settlement activities would also take place, between the regularly occurring ritual feasts?

It is impossible, at present, to assess whether any of these other tools would have been used in connection with activities associated with the feasting (or other rituals), but it should be pointed out that, in Northern Ireland, deposition of scrapers appear to have occurred in connection with activities at huge Late Neolithic ditches. In his report on the finds from Cashlandoo, Co. Antrim, the author wrote (Ballin 2007b): '*Recent evidence suggests that some ritual practices of the Irish later Neolithic period were centred around huge ditches, with some activities probably taking place within the enclosed area, and some in the ditch(es). Cashlandoo Ditch 018, as well as the ditch at Templecorran, Co. Antrim (Crothers 2000), both include metalled basal layers. The concentration of large end-scrapers at the bottom of Ditch 018 indicates that, most likely, some activities took place within the ditch, just as possible feasting seems to have taken place within the ditch at Whitepark Road, Co. Antrim (Ballin forthcoming f)*'. At Cashlandoo, half of all tools are simple edge-retouched pieces (expedient knives?), whereas one-quarter are scrapers, most of which display evident macroscopic use-wear. At Whitepark Road, approximately half of all deposited tools are used scrapers.

To achieve greater understanding of sites such as Airhouse and Overhowden, further research may have to be carried out. This problem is dealt with in the following chapter.

4. FUTURE PERSPECTIVES

Although there can be little doubt as to the classification of the Airhouse and Overhowden sites as unusual settlements, the functions of which are likely to be associated with the adjacent henge monument, a number of factors limit the scope of any analysis carried out on the sites via the recovered lithic finds. Many of these factors are products of the ways in which the assemblage was recovered and recorded (discussed in Chapter 1.3), and the analyst believes that revisiting the sites may prove fruitful.

Limited trial excavation was carried out at the Overhowden site (Atkinson 1950, 62), but according to the excavator, cultivation may have destroyed all features and structures. This, however, is by no means certain (no trial trenching was carried out at the Airhouse site), and renewed examination of both sites by the use of various forms of geo-physical approaches may reveal surviving features.

Even if all features have been destroyed, it may be possible to carry out distribution analysis by collecting all worked surface lithics next time the relevant fields are ploughed (they are presently under grass). It has been proven that, in flat non-sloping fields like those at Airhouse and Overhowden, horizontal artefact displacement tends to be limited (eg, Andersen 1972, Figs 10-11), and the resulting distribution patterns may prove highly informative in terms of prehistoric intra-site behaviour.

It is suggested to undertake systematic test-pitting across the two sites (this work can be carried out immediately, without waiting for the fields to be ploughed), first and foremost to shed light on one question: does the ploughsoil contain any lithic debitage or pottery? It is important to find out whether lithic debitage was produced and discarded at the sites, and thus, whether the many unusual tools were manufactured on-site or imported from other sites. As indicated through this paper, the author believes that the collection's lack of debitage is due to biased recovery, but this assumption ought to be tested. It is also important to retrieve any surviving cores, to find out whether those would mainly be Levallois-like pieces or whether they would belong to other core types. It is imperative to test whether any pottery is present, as this is a crucial piece of information in connection with the characterization of the sites and their activities. The stylistic definition of this pottery would then be relevant to the precise dating of the sites and, by association, their lithic assemblage.

A fuller understanding of the two sites and their combined assemblage would also benefit from further research of the Scottish Late Neolithic in general, and of the periods lithic material. It would be useful if more common domestic sites from this period were excavated, and their assemblages published. First and foremost, this would provide information as to whether the presently available assemblages are representative of the Scottish Late Neolithic reality, and in particular as to whether the composition of the available Late Neolithic assemblages from the Central Belt and southern Scotland (eg, the massive dominance of these collections by Yorkshire flint) is a product of those sites mainly being ritual or high-status sites.

Some Late Neolithic lithic assemblages are well-excavated and well-recorded but, due to either lack of publication or selective publication, they are not available for general comparative analysis. The sizeable pitchstone-cum-flint collection from Machrie Moor on Arran probably represents domestic settlement prior to the construction of the area's timber-built and stone circles, but the publication (Haggarty 1991) largely focused on the location's monuments and pottery. The lithic finds from Barnhouse were published in an equally selective manner, with focus being on the in-house artefact distribution, and it is basically impossible, on the basis of the lithics report, to quantify the collection, or any of its elements. Although both reports are very informative, in terms of the issues they have chosen to shed light on, both assemblages ought to be re-examined, re-classified/re-characterized, and re-published, to provide important comparative material of relevance to the analysis of the Scottish Late Neolithic at large.

In terms of the Late Neolithic lithic industry in general, a number of suggestions have been made in this paper, partly regarding the Levallois-like technique and the mental template behind it. The key suggestion was made, that the purpose behind this unusual reduction method was to produce broad flakes and slender blades from the same cores (for different tool forms), and although supporting evidence of this proposition does exist, the suggestion ought to be tested by the refitting of a suitable Late Neolithic assemblage (well-excavated/well-recorded, not excessively numerous, and including key artefact types, such as Levallois-like cores, crested pieces, finely faceted flakes and blades, PTDs, scrapers, and knives/serrated pieces).

The present paper also suggests the subdivision of PTDs into three main categories, instead of two: chisel-shaped arrowheads, oblique arrowheads and a deviating group (including Classes C2 and G). Although there are indications that some classes represent functional differences, and others chronological differences, a full understanding of the functional and chronological variation within this important implement category requires further research. New assemblages from Late Neolithic single-occupation sites need to be scrutinized and compared, possibly combining statistical and use-wear analyses with contextual analysis.

And, finally, many of the unusual tool forms recovered from the Airhouse and Overhowden sites would generally benefit from being exposed to high-powered microscopic use-wear analysis, which would allow the locations' on-site activity patterns to be assessed in a more authoritative fashion. Elements to be focused upon include the abraded edges of polished-edge implements, and the gloss of various knife forms, both of which were exposed to cursory examination in connection with the present paper.

BIBLIOGRAPHY

Andersen, S.H. 1972: Bro. En senglacial boplads på Fyn. *Kuml* 1972, 6-60.

Andersen, K. 1982: Mesolitiske flækker fra Åmosen, Sjælland. *Aarbøger for Nordisk Oldkyndighed og Historie* 1982, 5-18.

Armstrong, A. 1926: The Grimes Graves Problem in the Light of Recent Research. *Proceedings of the Prehistoric Society of East Anglia* 5, 91-136.

Armstrong, A. 1934: Grimes Graves, Norfolk. Report on the Excavation of Pit 12. *Proceedings of the Prehistoric Society of East Anglia* 7, 382-394.

Ashton, N., Dean, P., & McNabb, J. 1991: Flaked flakes: what, when and why? *Lithics* 12, 1-11.

Atkinson, R.J.C. 1950: Four New Henge Monuments in Scotland and Northumberland. *Proceedings of the Society of Antiquaries of Scotland* 84, 57-66.

Ballin, T.B. 1999a: Bipolar Cores in Southern Norway - Classification, Chronology and Geography. *Lithics* 20, 13-22.

Ballin, T.B. 1999b: *Kronologiske og Regionale Forhold i Sydnorsk Stenalder. En Analyse med Udgangspunkt i Bopladserne ved Lundevågen (Farsundprosjektet).* Unpublished PhD thesis, Institute of Prehistoric Archaeology, Aarhus University.

Ballin, T.B. 1999c: The Lithic Assemblage. *In* S. Speak and C. Burgess: Meldon Bridge: a centre of the third millenium BC in Peebleshire. *Proceedings of the Society of Antiquaries of Scotland* 129, 1-118.

Ballin, T.B. 2002a: Later Bronze Age Flint Technology: A presentation and discussion of post-barrow debitage from monuments in the Raunds area, Northamptonshire. *Lithics* 23, 3-28.

Ballin, T.B. 2002b: *The Lithic Assemblage from Dalmore, Isle of Lewis, Western Isles.* Unpublished report commissioned by Cardiff University.

Ballin, T.B. 2004a: The Mesolithic Period in Southern Norway: Material Culture and Chronology. *In* A. Saville (ed.): *Mesolithic Scotland and its Neighbours. The Early Holocene Prehistory of Scotland, its British and Irish Context, and some Northern European Perspectives*, 413-438. Edinburgh: Society of Antiquaries of Scotland.

Ballin, T.B. 2004b: The worked quartz vein at Cnoc Dubh, Isle of Lewis, Western Isles. Presentation and discussion of a small prehistoric quarry. *Scottish Archaeological Internet Reports (SAIR)* 11. [http://www.sair.org.uk/sair11/index.html.

Ballin, T.B. 2005: *The Lithic Assemblage from East Lochside, Kirriemuir, Angus.* Unpublished report commissioned by CFA Archaeology Ltd.

Ballin, T.B. 2006: Re-examination of the Early Neolithic pitchstone-bearing assemblage from Auchategan, Argyll, Scotland. *Lithics* 27.

Ballin, T.B. 2007a: The Lithic Assemblage. *In* T.B. Ballin, B.Ballin Smith, D. Swan, B. Will, D. Gallagher, & C. Smith: Additional artefacts from Townparks, Antrim Town. *Ulster Archaeological Journal* 66, 50-74.

Ballin, T.B. 2007b: The Lithic Assemblage from Cashlandoo, Co. Antrim, Northern Ireland. Unpublished report commissioned by ADS Archaeology Ltd.

Ballin, T.B. 2009: *Archaeological Pitchstone in Northern Britain. Characterization and interpretation of an important prehistoric source.* British Archaeological Reports British Series 476. Oxford: BAR Publishing.

Ballin, T.B. forthcoming a: The British Late Neolithic 'Levalloisian', and other operational schemas from the later prehistoric period. A discussion based on finds from the Stoneyhill Project, Aberdeenshire. Submitted to *Proceedings of Conference held by the British Neolithic Studies Group, at the British Museum 2005.*

Ballin, T.B. forthcoming b: Detailed characterisation and discussion of the pitchstone artefacts from Barnhouse in the light of recent research into Scottish archaeological pitchstone. *The New Orcadian Antiquarian Journal.*

Ballin, T.B. forthcoming c: The Felsite Quarry Complex of Northmaven. Observations from a fact-finding mission to Shetland. *Proceedings of Conference held by the British Neolithic Studies Group, at the British Museum 2005.*

Ballin, T.B. forthcoming d: The Flint Assemblage. *In* J. Harding & F. Healy: *Raunds Area Project. The Neolithic and Bronze Age Landscapes of West Cotton, Stanwick and Irthlingborough, Northamptonshire.* English Heritage Archaeological Reports. London: English Heritage.

Ballin, T.B. forthcoming e: The Lithic Assemblage. *In* P. Ashmore: Calanais, Isle of Lewis, Western Isles. *Scottish Archaeological Internet Reports (SAIR).*

Ballin, T.B. forthcoming f: The Lithic Assemblage. *In* S. McMullen: *Whitepark Road, Co. Antrim, Northern Ireland.*

Ballin, T.B. forthcoming g: The Lithic Assemblage. *In* J.C. & H.K. Murray: Garthdee Road, Aberdeen City, Aberdeenshire. *Proceedings of the Society of Antiquaries of Scotland.*

Ballin, T.B. forthcoming h: The Lithic Assemblage. *In* C. & H. Murray: *Excavations at Midmill, Kintore, Aberdeenshire.*

Ballin, T.B. forthcoming i: The Lithic Assemblage. *In* R. Toolis: Neolithic domesticity and other prehistoric anomalies: excavations at Laigh Newton, East Ayrshire. *Scottish Archaeological Internet Reports (SAIR)*.

Ballin, T.B. & Johnson, M. 2005: A Mesolithic Chert Assemblage from Glentaggart, South Lanarkshire, Scotland: Chert Technology and Procurement Strategies. *Lithics* 26, 57-86.

Ballin, T.B., Saville, A., Ward, T., & Tipping, R. forthcoming: A Late Hamburgian Flint and Chert Assemblage from Howburn in South Lanarkshire, Scotland.

Barber, M., Field, D. & Topping, P. 1999: *The Neolithic Flint Mines of England.* London: English Heritage.

Barclay, G. 1999: Cairnpapple Revisited 1948-1998. *Proceedings of the Prehistoric Society* 65, 17-46.

Barclay, G.J., & Russell-White, C.J. 1993: Excavations in the ceremonial complex of the fourth to second millennium BC at Balfarg/Balbirnie, Glenrothes, Fife. *Proceedings of the Society of Antiquaries of Scotland* 123, 43-210.

Becker, C.J. 1952: Die Nordschwedischen Flintdepots. *Acta Archaeologica* XXIII, 31-78.

Binford, L.R. 1983: *In Pursuit of the Past. Decoding the Archaeological Record.* London: Thames & Hudson.

Bordes, F., & Gaussen, J. 1970: Un Fonde de tente Magdalénien près de Mussidan (Dordogne). *Frühe Menschheit und Umwelt* 1, 313-29.

Bridgland, D.R., Saville, A. & Sinclair, J.M. 1997: New evidence for the origin of the Buchan Ridge Gravel, Aberdeenshire. *Scottish Journal of Geology* 33, 43-50.

Bryce, J. 1862: An Account of Excavations within the Stone Circles of Arran. *Proceedings of the Society of Antiquaries of Scotland* 4 (1860-62), 499-524.

Butler, C. 2005: *Prehistoric Flintwork.* Stroud: Tempus.

Caldwell, J.R. 1964: Interaction Spheres in Prehistory. *In* J.R. Caldwell & R.L. Hall (eds): *Hopewellian Studies.* Illinois State Museum, Scientific Papers 12(6), 133-143. Springfield: Illinois State Museum.

Callander, J.G. 1927: A Collection of Tardenoisian Implements from Berwickshire. *Proceedings of the Society of Antiquaries of Scotland* 69, 318-327.

Callander, J.G. 1928: A Collection of Stone Implements from Airhouse, Parish of Channelkirk, Berwickshire. *Proceedings of the Society of Antiquaries of Scotland* LXII (1927-28), 166-180.

Chan, B. 2009: Life Amongst the Rubbish: Middening and Conspicuous Consumption at Durrington Walls. *Internet Archaeology* 26.

Chan, B. forthcoming: The Lithic Assemblage. To form part of a future final report on the Stonehenge Riverside Project.

Clare, T. 1986: Towards a reappraisal of henge Monuments. *Proceedings of the Prehistoric Society* 52, 281-316.

Clark, J.G.D. 1932a: The Date of the Plano-Convex Flint-Knife in England and Wales. *The Antiquaries Journal* XII, 158-162.

Clark, J.G.D. 1932b: Discoidal Polished Flint Knives - Their Typology and Distribution. *Proceedings of the Prehistoric Society* VI, 40-54.

Clark, J.G.D. 1934a: The Curved Flint Sickle Blade of Britain. *Proceedings of the Prehistoric Society* VII, 67-81.

Clark, J.G.D. 1934b: Derivative Forms of the Petit Tranchet in Britain. *The Archaeological Journal* XCI, 32-58.

Clark, J.G.D. 1960: Excavations at the Neolithic Site at Hurst Fen, Mildenhall, Suffolk. *Proceedings of the Prehistoric Society* XXVI, 202-245.

Clarke, G., & Piggott, S. 1933: The Age of the British Flint Mines. *Antiquity* 7, 166-183.

Clarke, D.V., Cowie, T.G. & Foxon, A. 1985: *Symbols of Power at the Time of Stonehenge.* Edinburgh: National Museum of Antiquities of Scotland.

Corrie, J.M. 1916: Notes on Some Stone and Flint Implements Found near Dryburgh in the Parish of Mertoun, Berwickshire. *Proceedings of the Society of Antiquaries of Scotland* 50, 307-313.

Cowie, T.G. 1996: Torrs Warren, Luce Sands, Galloway: a report on archaeological and palaeoecological investigations undertaken in 1977 and 1979. *Transactions of the Dumfriesshire & Galloway Natural History & Antiquarian Society* LXXI, 11-105.

Crothers, N. 2000: Rescue excavations at Templecorran, Ballycarry, County Antrim. *Ulster Archaeological Journal* 59, 29-45.

Davidson, J.M. 1935: A Bronze Age Cemetery at Knappers, Kilbowie, Dumbartonshire. *Proceedings of the Society of Antiquaries of Scotland* 69, 352-382.

Durden, T. 1995: The production of specialised flintwork in the later Neolithic: a case study from the Yorkshire Wolds. *Proceedings of the Prehistoric Society* 61, 409-432.

Edinborough, K. 2005: Weapons of Maths Instruction: A Thousand Years of Technological Stasis in Arrowheads from the South Scandinavian Middle Mesolithic. *Papers from the Institute of Archaeology* 16, 50-58.

Evans, S.J. 1897: *The Ancient Stone Implements, Weapons and Ornaments of Great Britain.* London: Longmans, Green, and Co.

Fell, C.I. 1952: A Late Bronze Age Urnfield and Grooved-Ware Occupation at Honington, Suffolk. *Proceedings of the Cambridge Antiquarian Society* 45, 30-43.

Finlayson, B. 2007: Flint. *In* Hunter, J.: *Excavations at Pool, Sanday. A multi-period settlement from Neolithic to Late Norse times,* 389-403. Investigations in Sanday, Orkney 1. Kirkwall / Edinburgh: Orcadian Ltd. / Historic Scotland.

Fischer, A., Grønnow, B., Jønsson, J.H., Nielsen, F.O., & Petersen, C. 1979: *Stenaldereksperimenter i Lejre. Bopladsernes indretning.* Working Papers, The National Museum of Denmark 8. København: The National Museum of Denmark.

Foster, S.M. 2006: *Maeshowe and the Heart of Neolithic Orkney.* Edinburgh: Historic Scotland.

Gardiner, J. 2008: On the production of discoidal flint knives and changing patterns of specialist flint procurement in the Neolithic on the South Downs, England. *In*: Fokkens, H., Coles, B.J., van Gijn, A.L., Kleijne, J.P., Ponjee, H.H. & Slappendel, C.G. (eds.): *Between Foraging and Farming. An extended broad spectrum of papers presented to Leendert Louwe Kooijmans,* 235-246. Analecta Praehistorica Leidensia 40. Leiden: Leiden University.

Gibson, A. 2002: *Prehistoric Pottery in Britain and Ireland.* Stroud: Tempus.

Green, H.S. 1980: *The Flint Arrowheads of the British Isles. A detailed study of material from England and Wales with comparanda from Scotland and Ireland.* BAR British Series 75(i). Oxford: British Archaeological Reports.

Green, H.S. 1984: Flint arrowheads: Typology and interpretation. *Lithics* 5, 19-39.

Haggarty, A. 1991: Machrie Moor, Arran: recent excavations at two stone circles. *Proceedings of the Society of Antiquaries of Scotland* 121, 51-94.

Harding, A.F. 1987: Henge Monuments and Related Sites of Great Britain. Air Photographic Evidence and Catalogue. BAR British Series 175. Oxford: British Archaeological Reports.

Harding, J. 2000: Later Neolithic Ceremonial Centres, Ritual and Pilgrimage: the Monument Complex at Thornborough, North Yorkshire. *In* A. Ritchie (ed.): *Neolithic Orkney in its European Context,* 31-46.. McDonald Institute Monographs. Cambridge: McDonal Institute for Archaeological Research.

Harding, J. 2003: *Henge Monuments of the British Isles.* Stroud: Tempus Publishing Ltd.

Harding, I.C., Trippier, S., & Steele, J. 2004: The provenancing of flint artefacts using palynological techniques. In E.A. Walker, F. Wenban-Smith, & F. Healy (eds.): *Lithics in Action. Papers from the Conference Lithic Studies in the Year 2000.* Oxbow Books / Lithic Studies Society Occasional Paper 8. Oxford: Oxbow Books / Lithic Studies Society.

Healy, F. 1985: The struck flint. *In* Shennan, S.J., Healy, F. & Smith, I.: The Excavation of a Ring-Ditch at Tye Field, Lawford, Essex. *The Archaeological Journal* 142, 150-215.

Healy, F. 1993: Lithic Material. *In*: R. Bradley, P. Chowne, R.M.J. Cleal, F. Healy, & I. Kinnes: *Excavations on Redgate Hill, Hunstanton, Norfolk, and at Tattershall Thorpe, Lincolnshire.* East Anglian Archaeology Report 57, 28-39. Gressenhall: Field Archaeology Division, Norfolk Museums Service / Heritage Trust of Lincolnshire.

Healy, F. 1995: Prehistoric Material. *In*: Rogerson, A. (ed.) *A Late Neolithic, Saxon and Medieval Site at Middle Harling, Norfolk,* 32-40. A Late Neolithic, Saxon and Medieval Site at Middle Harling, Norfolk 74. Gressenhall: Field Archaeology Division, Norfolk Museums Services.

Healy, F. 1996: Lithics. *In*: Healy, F. (ed.) *The Fenland Project, 11. The Wissey Embayment: Evidence for Pre-Iron Age Settlement Accumulated prior to the Fenland Project,* 50-94. The Fenland Project, 11. The Wissey Embayment: Evidence for Pre-Iron Age Settlement Accumulated prior to the Fenland Project 78. Gressenhall: Field Archaeology Division, Norfolk Museums Services.

Henshall, A.S. 1963: *The Chambered Tombs of Scotland. Volume One.* Edinburgh: Edinburgh University Press.

Henshall, A.S. 1972: *The Chambered Tombs of Scotland. Volume Two.* Edinburgh: Edinburgh University Press.

Henson, D. 1982: *A study of flint as a raw material in prehistory, with an emphasis on Lincolnshire and Yorkshire.* Unpublished M. Phil. thesis. University of Sheffield.

Herne, A. 1991: The Flint Assemblage. In I. Longworth, A. Herne, G. Varndell & S. Needham, *Excavations at Grimes Graves, Norfolk 1972-1976. Fascicule 3, Shaft X: Bronze Age Flint, Chalk and Metal Working,* 21-93. London: British Museum Press.

Holgate, R. 1988: Neolithic Settlement of the Thames Basin. BAR British Series 194. Oxford: British Archaeological Reports.

Hope-Taylor, B. 1980: Balbridie ... and Doon Hill. *Current Archaeology* 72, 18-19.

Inizan, M.-L., Roche, H., & Tixier, J. 1992: *Technology of Knapped Stone.* Préhistoire de la Pierre Taillée 3. Meudon: Cercle de Recherches et d'Etudes Préhistoriques.

Johnson, M., & Ballin, T.B. 2006: Gaining Knowledge from the Ploughsoil: A Finds scatter from East Lochside, Kirriemuir. *Scottish Archaeology News* 51, 9.

Jones, A. 2007: Excavating art: recent excavations at the rock art sites at Torbhlaren, near Kilmartin, mid-Argyll, Scotland. *PAST* 57, 1-3.

Juel Jensen, H. 1994: *Flint Tools and Plant Working. Hidden Traces of Stone Age Technology. A use wear study of some Danish Mesolithic and TRB implements.* Århus: Aarhus University Press.

Kenmotsu, N. 1990: Gunflints: A Study. *Historical Archaeology* 24, **2**, 92-124.

Kenworthy, J.B. 1977: A reconsideration of the 'Ardiffery' finds, Cruden, Aberdeenshire. *Proceedings of the Society of Antiquaries of Scotland* 108, 80-93.

Kenworthy, J.B. 1981: The flint adze-blade and its cultural context. In J.N. Ritchie & H.C. Adamson: Knappers, Dunbartonshire: a reassessment. *Proceedings of the Society of Antiquaries of Scotland,* 189-193.

Kuhn, S.L. 1995: *Mousterian Lithic Technology. An Ecological Perspective.* Princeton, N.J.: Princeton University Press.

Lamdin-Whymark, H. forthcoming: The quartz assemblage. *In* A. Jones, D. Freeman, H. Lamdin-Whymark & A. Watson: *The Kilmartin Valley Project.* Oxford: Oxbow.

Larsson, L. 2004: Axeheads and fire – the transformation of wealth. *In* E.A. Walker, F. Wenban-Smith, & F. Healy (eds.) 2004: *Lithics in Action. Papers from the Conference Lithic Studies in the Year 2000.* Oxbow Books / Lithic Studies Society Occasional Paper 8. Oxford: Oxbow Books / Lithic Studies Society.

MacKay, R.R. 1948: Neolithic Pottery from Knappers Farm, near Glasgow. *Proceedings of the Society of Antiquaries of Scotland* 82 (1947-8), 234-237.

MacKie, E.W. 1973: Duntreath. *Current Archaeology* 36, 6-7.

Manby, T.G. 1974: *Grooved Ware Sites in Yorkshire and the North of England.* British Archaeological Reports British Series 9. Oxford: British Archaeological Reports.

Manby, T.G. 1979: Typology, materials, and distribution of flint and stone axes in Yorkshire. In T.H.M. Clough & W.A. Cummins (eds.) 1979: *Stone Axe Studies. Archaeological, Petrological, Experimental and Ethnographic*, 65-78. CBA Research Reports 23. London: Council for British Archaeology.

Mason, W.D. 1931: Prehistoric Man at Tweed Bridge, Selkirk. *Proceedings of the Society of Antiquaries of Scotland* 65, 414-417.

Megaw, J.V.S. & Simpson, D.D.A. 1979: *Introduction to British Prehistory. From the Arrival of Homo Sapiens to the Claudian Invasion.* Leicester: Leicester University Press.

Mellars, P. 1974: The Palaeolithic and Mesolithic. *In* C. Renfrew (ed.): British Prehistory – a New Outline, 41-99. London: Duckworth.

Mercer, R.J. 1981: The excavation of a late Neolithic henge-type enclosure at Balfarg, Markinch, Fife, Scotland, 1977-78. *Proceedings of the Society of Antiquaries of Scotland* 111, 63-171.

Mercer, R.J., Barclay, G.J., Jordan, D. & Russell-White, C.J. 1988: The Neolithic henge-type enclosure at Balfarg – a re-assessment of the evidence for an inco0mplte ditch circuit. *Proceedings of the Society of Antiquaries of Scotland* 118, 61-67.

Middleton, R. 2005: The Barnhouse Lithic Assemblage. *In* C. Richards (ed.) 2005: *Dwelling among the monuments. The Neolithic village of Barnhouse, Maeshowe passge grave and surrounding monuments at Stenness, Orkney*, 293-321. McDonald Institute Monographs. Cambridge: McDonald Institute for Archaeological Research.

Mitchell, A. 1889: Meeting Minutes. *Proceedings of the Society of Antiquaries of Scotland 23,* 18.

Moore, J.W. 1963: Excavations at Beacon Hill, Flamborough Head, East Yorkshire. *Yorkshire Archaeological Journal* CLXII, 191-202.

Mulholland, H. 1970: The Microlithic Industries of the Tweed Valley. *Transactions of the Dumfriesshire & Galloway Natural History & Antiquarian Society* 47, 81-110.

Peake, A. 1917: Further Excavations at Grimes Graves. *Proceedings of the Prehistoric Society of East Anglia* 2, 409-436.

Pierpoint, S. 1980: *Social Patterns in Yorkshire Prehistory 3500-750 B.C.* BAR British Series 74. Oxford: British Archaeological Reports.

Piggott, S. 1950: The Excavations at Cairnpapple Hill, West Lothian 1947-8. *Proceedings of the Society of Antiquaries of Scotland* 87 (1948-49), 68-123.

Piggott, S., & Simpson, D.D.A. 1971: Excavation of a Stone Circle at Croft Moraig, Perthshire, Scotland. *Proceedings of the Prehistoric Society*, 37, 1-15

Pitts, M.W. & Jacobi, R.M. 1979: Some Aspects of Change in Flaked Stone Industries of the Mesolithic and Neolithic in Southern Britain. *Journal of Archaeological Science* 6, 163-177.

Pryor, F. 1978: *Excavations at Fengate, Peterborough, England: The Second Report.* Royal Ontario Museum Archaeology Report 5. Toronto: Royal Ontario Museum.

Renfrew, C. 1977: Alternative Models for Exchange and Spatial Distribution. *In* T.K. Earle, & J.E. Ericson (eds.): *Exchange Systems in Prehistory.* Studies in Archaeology, 71-90. New York: Academic Press.

Rideout, J.S. 1997: Excavations of Neolithic enclosures at Cowie Road, Bannockburn, Stirling, 1984-5. *Proceedings of the Society of Antiquaries of Scotland* 127, 29-68.

Ritchie, J.N.G. 1976: The Stones of Stenness, Orkney. *Proceedings of the Society of Antiquaries of Scotland* 107, 1-60.

Ritchie, J.N.G., & Adamson, H.C. 1981: Knappers, Dunbartonshire: a reassessment. *Proceedings of the Society of Antiquaries of Scotland* 111, 172-204.

Roe, D.E. 1981: *The Lower and Middle Palaeolithic Periods in Britain.* The Archaeology of Britain. London, Boston and Henley: Routledge & Kegan Paul.

Russell, M. 2000: *Flint Mines in Neolithic Britain.* Stroud: Tempus Publishing Ltd.

Saville, A. 1981: *Grimes Graves, Norfolk. Excavations 1971/72: Volume II. The Flint Assemblage.* Department of the Environment Archaeological Reports 11. London: Her Majesty's Stationery Office.

Saville, A. 1995: GB 20 Den of Boddam near Peterhead, Grampian Region, Scotland. GB 21 Skelmuir Hill, Grampian Region, Scotland. Prehistoric exploitation of flint from the Buchan Ridge Gravels, Grampian region, north-east Scotland. *Archaeologia Polona* 33, 353-368.

Saville, A. 2005: Prehistoric Quarrying of a Secondary Flint Source: Evidence from North-East Scotland. *In*: Topping, P. & Lynott, M. (eds.): *The Cultural Landscape of Prehistoric Mines,* 1-13. The Cultural Landscape of Prehistoric Mines. Oxford: Oxbow Books.

Saville, A. 2006: Flint technology associated with extraction sites in north-east Scotland. *In*: Weisgerber, G. (ed.) *Stone Age - Mining Age. Proceedings of the VIII International Flint Symposium, Bochum, 1999.*, 449-454. Stone Age - Mining Age. Proceedings of the VIII International Flint Symposium, Bochum, 1999. 148. Bochum: Deutsches Bergbau-Museum Bochum.

Saville, A. 2008: Flint extraction and processing from secondary flint deposits in the north-east of Scotland in the Neolithic period. *In*: Allard, P., Bostyn, F., Giligny, F. & Lech, J. (eds.): *Flint Mining in Prehistoric Europe. Interpreting the archaeological records. European Association of Archaeologists, 12th Annual Meeting, Cracow, Poland, 19th-24th September 2006,* 1-10. BAR International Series 1891. Oxford: BAR Publishing.

Saville, A. in prep.: *The Late Neolithic Quarry Complex at Den of Boddham and Skelmuir Hill, Aberdeenshire.*

Schneiderman-Fox, F., & Pappalardo, A.M. 1996: A Paperless Approach Toward Field Data Collection: An Example from the Bronx. SAA Bulletin 14(1). [http://www.saa. org/publications/saabulletin/14-1/index.html.]

Schofield, A.J. 2000: *Managing lithic scatters. Archaeological guidance for planning authorities and developers.* London: English Heritage.

Scott, J.G. 1989: The hall and motte at Courthill, Dalry, Ayrshire. *Proceedings of the Society of Antiquaries of Scotland* 119, 271-278.

Scott, D.D., & Thiessen, T.D. 2005: Catlinite Extraction at Pipestone National Monument, Minnesota: Social and Technological Implications. In P. Topping. & M. Lynott (eds.): *The Cultural Landscape of Prehistoric Mines,* 140-154. Oxford: Oxbow Books.

Sharp, J. 1912: Notice of a Collection of Flint Arrowheads and Implements found on the Farm of Overhowden, in the Parish of Channelkirk, Berwickshire. *Proceedings of the Society of Antiquaries of Scotland* 46 (1911-12), 370-372.

Sheridan, A. 2007: From Picardie to Pickering and Pencraig Hill? New information on the 'Carinated Bowl Neolithic' in northern Britain. *Proceedings of the British Academy* 144, 441-492.

Smith, I.F. 1965: *Windmill Hill and Avebury. Excavations by A. Keiller, 1925-1939.* Oxford: Clarendon Press.

Smith, I.F. 1974: The Jet Bead from Fengate, 1972. *In* Pryor, F.: *Excavations at Fengate, Peterborough, England: The First Report,* 40-42. Royal Ontario Museum Archaeology Monograph 3. Toronto: Royal Ontario Museum.

Spicer, G. 2007: Perthshire rock art sheds light on Scotland's past. *24 Hour Museum – News.* [http:/www.24hourmuseum.org.uk/nwh_gfx_en/ART49620.html]

Stapert, D. & Johansen, L. 1999: Flint and pyrite: making fire in the Stone Age. *Antiquity* 73, 765-777.

Stevenson, R.B.K. 1948: 'Lop-sided' Arrow-heads. *Proceedings of the Society of Antiquaries of Scotland* LXXX (1946-48), 179-182.

Struever, S., & Houart, G.L. 1972: An Analysis of the Hopewell Interaction Sphere. *In* E.N. Wilmsen (ed.): *Social Exchange and Interaction,* 47-80. Museum of Anthropology, University of Michigan, Anthropological Papers 46. Ann Arbor: University of Michigan.

Suddaby, I., & Ballin, T.B. forthcoming: Stoneyhill, Aberdeenshire. *Scottish Archaeological Internet Reports (SAIR).*

Topping, P. 2005: Shaft 27 Revisited: An Ethnography. *In* Topping, P., & Lynott, M. (eds.) 2005: *The Cultural Landscape of Prehistoric Mines.* Oxford: Oxbow Books.

Vestergård, E. 2005: Vestergaards Matematiksider. Matematik for Gymnasiet og for Matematik-Interesserede. [http://www.matematiksider.dk/index.html].

Wainwright, G.J. 1979: *Mount Pleasant, Dorset: Excavations 1970-1971. Incorporating an account of excavations undertaken at Woodhenge in 1970.* Reports of the Research Committee of the Society of Antiquaries of London XXXVII. London: The Society of Antiquaries of London / Thames and Hudson.

Wainwright, G.J. & Longworth, I.H. 1971: *Durrinton Walls: Excavations 1966-1968.* Reports of the Research Committee of the Society of Antiquaries of London XXIX. London: The Society of Antiquaries of London / Thames and Hudson.

Warren, G. 2007: An Archaeology of the Mesolithic of Eastern Scotland. Deconstructing culture, constructing identity. *In* Waddington, C. & Pedersen, K. (eds.): *Mesolithic Studies in the North Sea Basin and Beyond,* 137-150. Oxford: Oxbow Books.

Wickham-Jones, C. 1981a: Flaked stone. *In* J.N.G. Ritchie & H.C. Adamson 1981: Knappers, Dunbartonshire: a reassessment. *Proceedings of the Society of Antiquaries of Scotland* 111, 193-198.

Wickham-Jones, C. 1981b: Report on the analysis of the flaked stone assemblage. *In* R.J. Mercer 1981: The excavation of a late Neolithic henge-type enclosure at Balfarg, Markinch, Fife, Scotland, 1977-78. *Proceedings of the Society of Antiquaries of Scotland* 111, 115-127.

Wickham-Jones, C. 1983: The industry of flaked stone from the henge monument at North Mains. *In* Barclay, G.J.: Sites of the third millennium bc to the first millennium ad at North Mains, Strathallan, Perthshire. *Proceedings of the Society of Antiquaries of Scotland* 113, 122-281.

Wickham-Jones, C. in prep.: Ness of Brodgar – notes on the flaked lithic assemblage, 2004-7. *In* N. Card: *Ness of Brodgar.*

Wickham-Jones, C., & Reed, D. 1993: The stone assemblage. *In* Barclay, G.J., & Russell-White, C.J.: Excavations in the ceremonial complex of the fourth to second millennium BC at Balfarg/Balbirnie, Glenrothes, Fife. *Proceedings of the Society of Antiquaries of Scotland* 123, 43-210.

Wilson, V. 1948: *East Yorkshire and Lincolnshire.* British Regional Geology 9. London: Natural Environment Research Council, Institute of Geological Sciences, Geological Survey and Museum / Her Majesty's Stationery Office.

Wilson, K.E., Longworth, I.H., & Wainwright, G.J. 1971: The Grooved Ware Site at Lion Point, Clacton. *British Museum Quarterly* 35, 93-124.

Yerkes, R.W. 2002: Hopewell Tribes: A Study of Middle Woodland Social Organization in the Ohio Valley. *In* W.A. Parkinson (ed.): *The Archaeology of Tribal Societies.* Archaeological Series 15, 227-245. Ann Arbor: International Monographs in Prehistory.

www.ingramcontent.com/pod-product-compliance
Lightning Source LLC
Chambersburg PA
CBHW061303270326
41932CB00029B/3460